Leader's Guide

LEADER'S GUIDE

"And the things you have heard me say in the presence of many witnesses entrust to reliable men who will also be qualified to teach others."

2 TIMOTHY 2:2

Operation Timothy

OT

CBMC Publications

The Christian Business Men's Committee is an international evangelical organization of Christian business and professional men whose primary purpose is to present Jesus Christ as Savior and Lord to other business and professional men and to train these men to carry out the Great Commission.

CBMC of USA is a nondenominational, non-profit Christian ministry supported by gifts from people committed to reaching and discipling business and professional men for Jesus Christ.

More information may be obtained by writing:

Christian Business Men's Committee of USA
1800 McCallie Avenue
Chattanooga, Tennessee 37404
1-800-575-2262

Operation Timothy is an investigative Bible study with the goal of helping people to grow spiritually. It has been designed to serve as a link with the Living Proof I and II Video Series.
For more information, call 1-800-575-2262

Isa Williams, graphic designer

Operation Timothy Leader's Guide – ISBN # 0-945292-06-6

Contents

OPERATION TIMOTHY LEADER'S GUIDE

Operation Timothy is an investigative Bible study with the goal of helping people to grow spiritually. This Leader's Guide is designed for use by a facilitator in a one-on-one or small group situation as a link with the Living Proof I and II video series. The material covers books 1 through 4. They are —

1. **Finding the Way**
2. **Knowing the Truth**
3. **Living with Power**
4. **Making a Difference**

HOW TO USE THIS GUIDE

This Leader's Guide follows the format of Operation Timothy Books 1 through 4. It is designed to be used in a one-on-one situation or small group setting. It may be used with new Christians or with those who are investigating the claims of Christ. Originally designed for application in men's groups, the materials have been written to exclude language which may limit its use with women as well.

The material has been written and designed to keep preparation time to a minimum. Our purpose in doing so is to provide additional time for you as the leader to pray for and interact with your Timothy. Our approach is not content vs. relationship, rather we encourage a balance of both.

The Leader's Guide is arranged to give you a visual picture of where you are. On each page you will find icons corresponding with Timothy's study guide, margin notes with helpful teaching tips, and much, much more.

In an effort to improve our materials continually, we encourage your suggestions and observations. Our goal is to serve the Christian community at-large, as well as members of CBMC here in the United States and abroad by providing high quality, cost effective materials to reach and disciple men and women for Christ.

OPERATION TIMOTHY: THE PURPOSE

You are embarking on something BIG…the awesome privilege of being involved in the PLANS OF GOD. People are at the heart of God — He desires a relationship with us and a growing intimacy.

God has specifically chosen us to be the means of being His light and extending His love to His world. It is not an option.

God has an intense desire for people to be rightly related to Him: — "he desires all men to be saved and come to the knowledge of Him." (I Timothy 2:4.) God did not choose angels or His creation to articulate this good news of Jesus Christ. And God did not choose a few gifted individuals to be His messengers. He chose every believer to be a witness of His glory in their words, in their conduct, in their attitudes — in summation, their very lives. (Matthew 5:16)

Yet, just as babies need to grow and be taught how to communicate, so it is with new believers. This growth and teaching of new believers is at the heart of discipleship. Discipleship is God's means of growing and maturing a new Christian to accomplish the following: for each individual to grow in an intimate relationship with his Lord, to be a life witness of Christ to a searching world, to offer love and care to the hurting and desperate, and to be interdependent in meeting each others' needs. Operation Timothy is not just a curriculum or program that teaches information and principles. OT is an opportunity for you to enter into a relationship with another believer or seeker, either one-on-one or with several in a small group. The purpose is that each might grow in intimacy with God and catch the vision of multiplying disciples. With each person indwelt by Christ, God uses them to reach the next generation. In impacting the next generation God's glory is extended to the end of the earth and to the end of time. So, the process of OT is something big, larger than you, and yet, it allows you to leverage your impact in this world.

> The process of OT is something big, larger than you, and yet, it allows you to leverage your impact in this world.

Multiplied thousands have entered into the OT process which has dramatically changed their lives and their vision. Don't hesitate to enter as a disciple or as a discipler. God will touch you, mold you and use you for His kingdom purpose.

In Isaiah 60:22, God promises the people of Israel to make the the least and the smallest of them a mighty nation. He is looking for people who will love, follow and obey Him. It is this promise and, moreover, this vision, that has fired the souls of many to enter into the lifechanging process of Operation Timothy, that "one may become a THOUSAND." Fruitfulness is the result of a life yielded to God to be used by Him. Do you desire this fruitfulness? The only requirement is to be a little small one in the Hands of God, and He will hasten it in His time.

CBMC and the Relational Approach

More than sixty years ago, Christian Business Men's Committee of USA recognized the problem. The leaders realized that you make changes through leadership, and, as the saying goes, the business of our country is business. CBMC sought to make a powerful impact on our nation — and beyond, on the world — through the business community and the relationships around which they are built.

CBMC takes the battle into the world's marketplace and neighborhoods. And rather than use formulas or classes, it presents the gospel through relationships.

To that end, this Leader's Guide will often suggest questions to consider that relate content to context, and learning to life. This will help keep you both from merely intellectualizing your experience. This is practical stuff. You will study and discuss such topics as faith in the home, the handling of money and "taking it to work."

The Goal of the Process

Keep the "big picture" in mind during each session. What is the bottom line? The central purpose of the lesson? As you approach each lesson, look for opportunities to connect a human being with Christ. How often do we go about a full slate of Christian activities without sharing the company of the One who is at the center of them? For the process to be effective, it must begin with you. You must be connected to Christ. Be sure you are in the Word of God on a daily basis.

Tell me and I forget; Show me and I remember; Involve me and I understand.

SIOUX INDIAN PROVERB

The fact is, you cannot teach the reality of Christ if He is not a reality to you. Timothy needs to see Jesus living in and through another human. It will give him the desire to experience what he sees being lived out before him.

PRINCIPLES OF EFFECTIVE DISCIPLESHIP

1. THE PRINCIPLE OF THE SPIRITUAL GROWTH PROCESS

As believers, we are called to make disciples (Matt. 28:19-20). If we examine Christ's command in Matthew 28, we see that evangelism and discipleship are one process. The Bible uses the metaphors of farming and parenting to describe it. When the Scriptures speak of evangelism, almost without exception, it uses the picture of a farmer tilling the soil, planting seed and harvesting the produce.

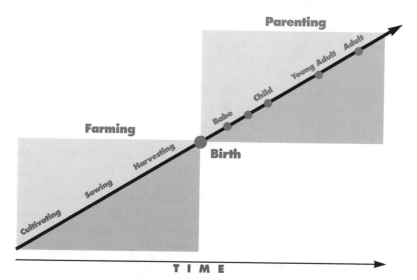

Parenting begins after harvesting. For example, the apostle Paul writes, "My dear children, for whom I am again in the pains of childbirth until Christ has formed you." To the church in Thessalonica he writes, "But we were gentle among you, like a mother caring for her children... for you know that we dealt with each of you as a father deals with his own children..." Peter spoke of, "newborn babies." John repeatedly addressed his readers as "dear children." And Hebrews talks about spiritual "infancy" and the importance of moving to "adulthood."

As farmers, we cultivate relationships with non-believers, allowing them to witness first-hand the power of a changed life. Once a person becomes a believer, our role changes to that of spiritual parent. Just as with any newborn, spiritual babes are fragile and require a lot of time and energy. But as we continue the life-on-life process, modeling the way and helping the young believer grow into adulthood, our initiative becomes less as we allow him to flourish and eventually reproduce. This is not a program. It's a long process.

For deeper understanding of this critical process, complete Lesson 4 in Book 4, *Making a Difference* before you begin meeting with Timothy.

2. THE PRINCIPLE OF SPIRITUAL FARMING

Spiritual farming consists of three phases: cultivating, sowing and harvesting.

CULTIVATING – Before we can sow seed, we must break up the hard ground, removing rocks, roots and other debris. If the soil is the human heart, God must remove obstacles and prepare it to receive the Word.

Cultivation begins with a relationship, and relationships work through common ground. Activities, sports, computers, cooking, music — all can become the common ground of a new relationship. In I Corinthians 9:19-23, Paul tells how he related to different kinds of people in order to lead them to Christ. He met people at their point of need. Jesus did, too. He went to them. In doing so, He was known as a "friend of sinners." He didn't think that was such a bad thing. Our call is to do the same.

SOWING – The goal of sowing is to bring the unbeliever to a place where they ask the question, "who is Jesus?" It may take years. Along the way, believers must be patient and consistent. But when the unbelieving friend is comfortable enough with us, and they like what they see, we can sow the Word. Remember, we are to be "salt and light," (Matthew 5:13-14). Salt causes thirst. Light illuminates. Operation Timothy is designed to sow the Word.

HARVESTING – We can cultivate and sow for years and never see a harvest. We must leave that to God. Paul tells us in I Corinthians 3:6-7 that, "I planted, Apollos watered, but God was causing the growth. So then, neither the one who plants nor the one who waters is anything, but God who causes the growth." This is a long process. It takes time to turn hard, rocky clay into fertile, crop-producing soil. As we walk in obedience, we still share in the joy of that person coming into the kingdom of God. When we see a person come to know Christ, the metaphor shifts from that of farmer to that of parent.

3. THE PRINCIPLE OF SPIRITUAL PARENTING (LIFE ON LIFE)

Most people in western culture approach the subject of discipleship in a systematic, logical manner. We create an agenda, formulate a plan, and launch out — often oblivious to the needs of the person with whom we are attempting to share our life in Christ.

The approach of Jesus followed the patterns indigenous to ancient Palestine. As a Rabbi (teacher), Jesus spent time with his followers. His disciples had the opportunity to observe his reactions to the rich, the poor, the priests, and the politicians. He was constantly asking questions, forcing them to think through choices and weigh events against the teachings of Scripture.

Jesus was very practical, too. They discussed the purpose and use of money, the importance of family, and the role of government. For over three years, His disciples were engaged in a life-on-life course on how to live for God in a fallen world.

For the Duration

Life-on-life discipleship is a long-term commitment. This kind of relationship requires sacrifice and may seem too costly to some. Those who see the end from the beginning possess the vision necessary for success. In His work with the twelve, Jesus did not see his ministry in their lives as something that could be put on the calendar or measured in terms of hours, days or weeks. In the three years He ultimately spent with his disciples, Jesus' devotion to them was absolute, His commitment was unlimited.

It is interesting to note that Jesus took into account changing roles and situations. For example, He dealt with Peter in a different manner than He did with Bartholomew. As a spiritual parent, you will be wise to keep in mind the stages of spiritual growth in Timothy. Infants, children, and adolescent children of God require flexibility with schedules and materials. If you have children of your own, you will see the parallels. As you deal with Timothy, begin with the patience required of a parent with a new-born and adjust your expectations as growth occurs.

Jim Peterson states: "Our tendency is to create programs for discipleship and offer them to people as a substitute for parental care. We put people through a prescribed curriculum and expect that to take care to their needs. It doesn't work. It doesn't work because their primary need at this stage is not for information. Caring relationships are far more important to the early stages.

"New Christians need a meaningful relationship with spiritual parents. It's a primary spiritual need, along with their need for Scripture, If study guides are used, they need to be carefully chosen. They must guide people into Scripture, and the content of those guides must truly correspond with needs. If we fail to connect these matters of relationships and appropriate content, the new Christian will often just stall out in his or her growth. They might do the studies and show up with all the right answers, but still flunk the test in true spiritual growth."

> As a spiritual parent, you will be wise to keep in mind the stages of spiritual growth in Timothy.

Care must be taken not to extend this idea of spiritual parent-hood to the point where one person virtually takes over the life of another. This kind of control becomes bizarre and creates dependency rather than producing adulthood. Paul said, "Not that we lord it over your faith, but we work with you for your joy, because it is by faith you stand firm."

4. THE PRINCIPLE OF REPRODUCTION AND MULTIPLICATION (THE NEW MATH)

In the first pages of the Bible we discover one of the purposes of man on earth: reproduction and multiplication. The same is true in the spiritual dimension.

A Spiritual Baby Boom

We see in the New Testament roots of the spiritual family tree to which all believers are connected. Jesus began with twelve, taught and lived the principles of a life lived under God's authority. We are the spiritual descendants of The Twelve.

Of course, the principle of exponential growth does not require the number twelve. For example, if you as an individual were to reach and cultivate two new believers over a two year period, and continued this practice (and they did likewise), in 25 years you would have produced over a thousand spiritual descendants.

Isaiah 60:22 says, "The least of you will become a thousand, the smallest a mighty nation." And remember, while some might not be faithful, others will reach more than two — and many will have families that number in the tens of thousands. It is a formula for changing the world.

Fruitful Labors

In John 15:16, Jesus tells His followers to, "Go and bear fruit." A fully loaded apple tree is the result of one small seed. Who knows where those seeds will scatter and take root? How many new trees will grow as a result of that first small, seemingly insignificant seed?

We will never see the fruits of our labors in our life time. Yes, we will enjoy the fellowship and companionship of the first seeds, and first fruit, but long after we are gone, countless others will follow.

Just as parents enjoy the rich rewards and the unique experience that comes with raising children, we as spiritual parents do the same. In the end, we find ourselves closer to God, more in line with what He desires during our stay on earth.

> A fully loaded apple tree is the result of one small seed. Who knows where those seeds will scatter and take root?

5. THE PRINCIPLE OF BEING AN INSIDER

The decision to follow Christ seriously carries radical, even traumatic, implications. It is a watershed in one's life. When the difference between the church and the world is so extreme, the tendency is for the Christian to bail out of society completely, seeking refuge in the Christians' cloistered fellowship. In I Corinthians 7, the Apostle Paul repeats three times the command for the believers to remain in the situation in which God has called them. We are instructed to stay put and make a difference where we are.

Bloom Where You're Planted

The implications are significant for Timothy. If married to an unsaved spouse, remain in the marriage. If working in the midst of a pagan culture or a spiritually hostile work environment, stay there and make a difference. This may seem to be a radical prescription for a young, fragile Christian. Again, the tendency of new and excited converts will be to immerse themselves in activities and Christian fellowship. Yet, it is just this kind of young believer, with a fresh commitment and reckless enthusiasm, who most often has the greatest impact for Christ. The rest of us, sadly enough, become more and more enmeshed in activities that take us deeper into fellowship with other Christians, while at the same time, putting distance between ourselves and the place God has planted us to reach with the good news. Paul was aware that new Christians were in a position to influence their culture from the inside out and to reach others in the marketplace.

As you share your life with Timothy, you may need to make some effort to encourage him not to "bail out" as a player. The tension will come as a result of Timothy's drive to purity while attempting to maintain the vital position for influence with old friends and associates.

A Child Shall Lead Them

It is ironic, is it not, that God in his wisdom is positioning infants to accomplish His greatest works of evangelism! These people have not been branded as fanatics. They continue to have the trust of the crowd. Your role is to watch over, to counsel, and encourage Timothy. Encourage Timothy to begin sharing the gospel with others now — explain that there is no need to wait until someone has completed several discipleship courses to start telling others about Jesus Christ. The Great Commission begins now.

In summary, we as believers are to serve on the "inside" in our culture and as active agents of change. And we do it now, not tomorrow or next week.

6. THE PRINCIPLE OF BEING A LABORER

In Matthew 9:36, we pick up a conversation Jesus was having with the twelve. The Bible says, "…He had compassion on them, because they were harassed and helpless, like sheep without a shepherd." Turning to His inner circle of disciples, the Lord continued, "…the harvest is plentiful but the workers are few. Ask the Lord of the harvest, therefore, to send out workers into his harvest field." (vs. 37-38)

Each individual life is compared to a crop needing to be tended, watered, prepared, and ultimately, reaped. Send out workers! This is God's pressing desire. With more people walking the earth than at any time in history, the harvest field is almost beyond imagination. There is an urgent need to pray that God will use us to equip, train, and send out more laborers. That is the essence of discipleship.

Go With the Flow

To become an effective discipler we must first be a disciple. There is always the temptation to feed others while depriving ourselves. However, if we constantly give, and do not receive, we will dry up and have little to give the cause of Christ. Therefore, it is of vital importance as you instruct and encourage a young Christian that you continue to seek God personally, stay grounded in His Word, develop your prayer life, and stay close to other growing Christians.

Eight Qualities of an Effective Discipler

Some doubt they have the skills or time to give themselves to becoming a discipler. Ultimately, it is a matter of the will and of obedience. Just as few of us feel ready to become biological parents, few *feel* ready to take on the nurture and care of a spiritual infant. The following qualities are the ingredients of an effective disciple maker:

LOVE OF GOD: The quality of an infectious love of God.

LOVE OF PEOPLE: The ability to help Timothy learn to love others as God does.

VISION: The ability to see Timothy as he can be, while accepting him where he is.

FAITHFULNESS: The ability to depend on God to be consistent.

DEPENDABILITY: The availability that causes Timothy to see you as someone to be trusted.

HEART OF A TEACHER: The ability to look for a teachable moment.

SERVANTHOOD: The quality of a humble heart, the willingness to sacrifice for Timothy's needs.

DURABILITY: A heart that says, "Whatever it takes."

7. THE PRINCIPLE OF SPIRITUAL TRANSFORMATION

Authentic Christian growth comes from the inside and works its way
to the surface —just the opposite of the manner we so often seek to
impose. When we foolishly measure a new Christian's progress
based on the trappings of spirituality (the right words, the correct
do's and don'ts), we settle for the good over the best, the expedient
over the extraordinary. It is the heart motivation that must change.
And that revolutionary kind of transformation takes place on three
fronts: world view, values, and behavior.

Spiritual change starts from within — it is a transformation. There are three components
with which to deal: world view, values, and behavior. Discipleship focuses first on
world view — my view of God and God's view of the world. This is where I answer
the big questions of life: how did I get here? where am I going? who is in charge? My
answer to these will affect my value system — what is important to me, what I will die
for, etc. My behavior, then, is a direct outgrowth of my world view and my values. Much
of spiritual growth in the past focused on behavior first: "the do's and don'ts" (do I
smoke, dance, drink, etc?). We tried to clean people up on the outside (reformation) without a change on the inside (transformation). This spiritual transformation begins with
God. Philippians 1:6 says it best: "He who began a good work in me will perfect it…"
It is the role of the Holy Spirit and God's Word to establish and build us spiritually.
"Christ is my life" is the ultimate goal in our walk (Colossians 3:4). It is a life yielded
to and drawing upon the Spirit of God within us. God's role is to grow us to maturity;
our role as a spiritual parent is to guide, counsel, and care for the new believer.

8. THE PRINCIPLE OF THE THREE C'S: COMPETENCE, CHARACTER, AND COMMUNITY

It is the journey that brings maturity. There are no shortcuts, no substitutes, no way to
pay or earn a better position along the path. Maturity takes time, commitment, and
sacrifice. Jim Petersen, in his book *Lifestyle Discipleship*, discusses three central issues
around which spiritual maturity is manifest: competence, character, and community.

Competence

This refers to the basics of living and working as a Christian. How does a Christian
handle this or that situation? Where are the answers to be found? How can I communicate with God? It is true that a lifetime in God's Word is not enough time to understand
its depth and meaning. However, we need to be competent in our knowledge of the
Scripture, "correctly handling the word of truth." (2 Timothy 2:15) Beyond that, we must
be competent in the area of skill — how to counsel as well as listen; to articulate the
gospel and basic Christian truth; to function in a small group setting, and many more.

Character

Character has been defined as "who you are when no one is looking." This means that our behavior is to be pleasing to God who is watching. It is a lifetime pursuit, and may be the most difficult of all areas in which a Christian builds spiritual maturity. Not only is God watching, so is the world. Character grows through suffering. It is a quality that is not so much built as it is forged.

Community

The final issue is that of community. In a culture characterized by the "rugged individualist," we are duped to believe that we can do this alone — just me and God in divine fellowship. The truth is that God designed a better way. We are to do it together. He created us for fellowship. Since the beginning, God has said that it is not good for humans to be alone. (Genesis 2:18) We need each other.

Spiritual maturity is always framed in the context of community. It is here that we find and exercise our gifts, and look to our brothers and sisters to supply the gifts we do not possess. It is here that we find humility, receive rebuke and correction. When we become discouraged, and God seems far off, it is often through the community that God reaches out to us. Here is affirmation and encouragement and accountability. Community begins for Timothy in the context of your one-on-one relationship, but Timothy will have needs you will not be able to supply — it will take a friend, or a small group, or a church fellowship to serve the needs of a new believer. Good disciplers help find a place where roots can grow.

9. THE PRINCIPLE OF "THE BALANCED LIFE" — THE THREE DEVOTIONS

Finally, we must talk about maintaining a balanced focus for our lives and ministry. God has created man with three overarching needs: a need for God, a need to be involved in a cause bigger than himself, and a need for one another. For man (individually and corporately) to be at peace and be fruitful here on earth, these needs must be met and must be in balance. We are called to be devoted to Christ (expression of the first commandment "love God with all your heart, mind, soul… Matthew 22:37,38), to be devoted to one another (this is the second greatest commandment that "you love one another"…Matthew 22:39), and to be devoted to the gospel (The Great Commission: "Go therefore and make disciples…" Matthew 28:19,20).

These devotions must be balanced; if we neglect one of them, we will not be fruitful over the long haul. If, as an individual, a team, or a church, we neglect devotion to the gospel, we will become self-focused and self-absorbed, not reaching out to others. If we misuse the concept of love for one another, we produce hurt, and we use people for our own means. Or, if we aren't devoted wholeheartedly to Christ, we miss it all and walk in the flesh.

We want to see Timothy grow in these areas as we disciple him/her. This balance will help Timothy grow up and give away his life, rather than holding onto it. He will truly be one who becomes a thousand (Isaiah 60:22).

GETTING STARTED

You've heard the challenge. But four words come to mind: Where do I start?

Where do I find Timothy?

Standing on the Mount of Olives, the disciples watched their leader disappear into the clouds and felt just as overwhelmed as you may feel today. But Jesus had made things clear and concise. Here is how Jesus said to do it: *You will be my witnesses in Jerusalem (Acts 1:8)* Today Jerusalem, tomorrow the world. Jerusalem was not the hometown of any of the disciples. They were practically tourists, having followed Jesus there. He ordered them to start here and now. Urgency is, therefore, a part of the equation. There is also, in this statement, an emphasis on the marketplace, where the people are: the Jerusalems of any particular era.

Steps in finding Timothy

1. Ask God to make you sensitive and attentive. Look for growing relationships between you and particular friends and acquaintances. Evaluate the "chemistry" you share (or lack) with some that you know.

> One note of caution: in meeting one-on-one, a man should always meet with another man; a woman with another woman.

2. Survey the social landscape around you. Cultivate several relationships and see where they lead. Ask different acquaintances to lunch. Enlarge your circles of friendship.
3. "Raise the Flag" from time to time. That is, mention in a sentence your faith in Christ. Observe the response. Try telling a faith story ("How God helped me through the time when…"). Afterward, take some time for "gardening:" watch what breaks the surface after you've planted these seeds. It may take a few days or a few weeks, or longer.
4. Consider both non-Christians as well as young believers. The most likely person is the one you lead to Christ personally.
5. If you feel God leading you to a specific person, spend some quality time with him/her without proposing the greater commitment of a study. Invite this person to dinner. Do something recreational together over a weekend. Build informality and levity into the relationship from the beginning (it will serve you well later).

How do I invite Timothy to do Operation Timothy?

Ask general questions about Timothy's background, including spiritual, emotional and physical areas of life, as you spend time together. Ask God to give you discernment to recognize when He has prepared Timothy. Ask Him for courage to ask Timothy to investigate the Scriptures together at that time. Reflect on the "Spiritual Awareness Chart" below, asking God to give you insight into where Timothy is in his spiritual journey.

SPIRITUAL AWARENESS CHART

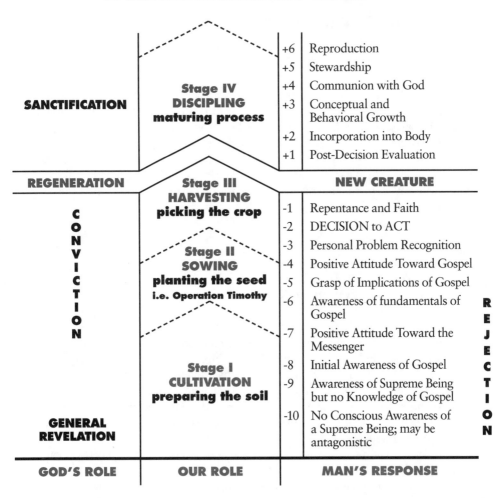

GOD'S ROLE	OUR ROLE	MAN'S RESPONSE

Don't rush or pressure. Notice the different phases of each stage in the chart. One person may quickly move through these; it may take another person years to change from an antagonistic attitude to a mere willingness to discuss spiritual issues. As mere, finite human beings, we cannot see into another person's heart and know for certain where they are spiritually at any time, but God's Spirit does give discernment into Timothy's spiritual needs.

If Timothy seems open, show him the Operation Timothy books. Explain that he/she will be able to investigate personally what the Bible says about various topics. Point out a few topics from the Table of Contents in Book 1. Ask Timothy if he/she would like to meet regularly to discuss these issues. If Timothy agrees, set a time and place to meet and give him Book 1, *Finding the Way*. Ask him to complete the lesson before your appointment. Show him the question-and-answer format and the printed Scriptures in the text.

Where and when?

Time and place are important considerations. Find out about Timothy's schedule. A weekly lunch appointment can work, but time will be constrained. Remember, you need 90 minutes. Breakfast might be better. Most of us are sharper in the morning. An evening, over a simple dinner, can be an excellent time because Timothy will tend to be under less pressure to be somewhere else. If Timothy is single, this might be your best option.

Where should you meet? Be creative. Think about a good environment for talking and praying. The clatter of a diner can be distracting. Your office is a possibility. Come to an agreement on the best time and place for both of you, and commit to them.

Here are some other points to consider as you begin. Be sure you do some of the sharing, rather than simply asking all the questions. Be open and transparent. Balance personal sharing with discussion of the Scriptural truths in the lessons. You might fail to finish a lesson in one week. Timothy might have special needs — it's okay to complete the lesson the next week. Review the previous lesson each week and any other lessons that you feel Timothy may need to be reminded of. Try to close with prayer. Thank God for what has been learned as well as shared; ask His guidance in the issues you discussed.

A NOTE ABOUT PRAYER

Prayer is the time you and Timothy spend directly in the presence of God. Keep in mind the importance of that statement, and avoid falling into the "punctuational prayer" trap: using it as bookends for a meeting. Timothy is learning to talk to God through your model. You'll do most of the praying in the beginning, with Timothy picking up his share as time progresses. Be sure to use language that Timothy understands.

How is the weekly meeting structured?

A typical 90 minute OT session will look something like this:

Arrival and welcome	(5 minutes)
Fellowship and sharing	(15 minutes)
Scripture memory (Begins in Book 2)	(10 minutes)
Review of previous lessons	(15 minutes)
Discuss major topic	(30 minutes)
Assignment	(5 minutes)
Prayer	(10 minutes)

No session will be exactly the same. Be flexible, but avoid the temptation to let fellowship stretch out too long, unless Timothy is in a crisis and needs time to talk.

How do I ask questions?

Study Jesus' use of questions and how He guided people toward the truth through them. A good question compels the listener to discover the truth for himself or herself. Let's look at some different types of questions:

LEADING QUESTION: "Isn't God good?" This type predetermines response and is a dead end to meaningful discussion and education.

LIMITING QUESTION: "In what three ways is God good, according to this passage?" There are good uses for this type — it focuses direction, but the questioner seems to take the role of an examiner rather than that of a co-explorer.

OPEN QUESTION: "What can we learn about God in this passage?" Now there is room for Timothy to do some of the work and provide interpretation. The question provokes interest and compels a thoughtful response.

WIDE-OPEN QUESTION: "Any other interesting truths in this passage?" A good concluding question, which allows Timothy to add something new from his own observation.

How should I prepare for a session?

1. Pray every day during the week.
2. Keep up with Timothy. Avoid letting your weekly meeting be your only contact.
3. Study the Leader's Guide as well as the Operation Timothy lessons. Timothy will learn to be prepared as he sees you setting a good example.
4. Expect God to do great things. Just when we feel most inadequate, or have questions about whether Timothy is really "getting it," God will prove that He is at work. Not all of Timothy's growth will be visible. Remember: growth depends not on your weakness or strength, but His strength.

May God bless you richly
as you and Timothy embark together!

SAMPLE LESSON PLAN

On a separate piece of paper or in your notebook, write out your own personal lesson plan for each week's discussion. Choose the suggested questions and illustrations from the Leader's Guide that you want to cover with Timothy and add questions of your own. Write these out in the order in which you want to cover them in your session. Each lesson highlights several key questions. Be sure you cover these thoroughly.

Make copies of the OT Diary on page 22 and 23. Keep notes on Timothy's progress, needs, etc.

BOOK 1, CHAPTER 1: The Bible: Believe It or Not

Sample Outline

Q. What is your church or spiritual background? What was your parent's view of the Bible, church, God when you were growing up? Now? On a scale of 1-10 how would you describe your familiarity with the Bible?

Key questions will appear in purple type.

PAGE 6: What was new/significant about how the Bible is organized?

PAGE 7: Share the "Plumbline" illustration.

PAGE 8: What was the significance of these Bible stories to you as a child? What do they say to you today?

PAGE 10: Reactions to "10 pennies" illustration.

PAGE 11: Discuss diagram.

PAGE 13: Additional questions about Luke 24:13-32.

VERSE 19: How does the questioner describe Jesus of Nazareth?

VERSE 20: How did the present rulers feel about this?

VERSE 21: How long ago had the crucifixion taken place?

VERSE 22: Who were the first people to discover the empty tomb?

VERSE 23: What was the word that they brought back?

VERSE 24: What happened then?

VERSES 25-27: What resource did Jesus use to explain these events to the two men? What is the significance of these statements to you?

VERSES 28-32: What is your reaction to these verses? Anything stand out to you? Why do you think they did not recognize Jesus at first?

PAGE 14: For you, what were the two most interesting points in this chapter? Why? What other questions do you have about the Bible? Do you own a Bible?

Share illustrations about Sir Isaac Newton, Design Argument if needed.

Ask Timothy about prayer background. Comfortable praying out loud? List requests, then pray.

OPERATION TIMOTHY DIARY

The purpose of this diary is to record information that will help you be more effective in prayer and ministry to your "Timothy." Each week, after your session, enter any new information that will help you work with him/her. *Make copies of these pages as needed.*

Name _____ Nickname _____

Address _____ City _____ Zip _____

Home Phone _____ Business Phone _____

Age _____ Birthdate _____ Spouse's Name _____

Children's Names & Ages _____

Present Job_____ How long?_____

Previous Work _____

Hobbies _____

Other Personal Information _____

_____

_____

_____

Sessions Notes: Progress? Does he need help with major concepts, family issues, application of principles, prayer, Scripture memory, etc.?

_____

_____

_____

_____

_____

_____

_____

_____

_____

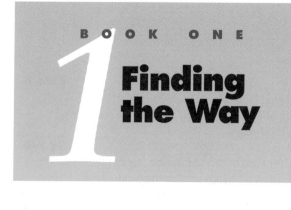

BOOK ONE

1 Finding the Way

The stairway illustrates the process of spiritual growth — one step at a time. <u>Finding the Way</u> investigates the credibility of the Bible and the relevancy of the claims of Christ. It is geared toward seekers and new Christians. Scriptural verses are printed out in the text itself. The goal of this first of four books is to whet Timothy's appetite to become a life-long student of the Scriptures, not to force a decision by the end of chapter 6. Many will be ready to begin a relationship with Christ. Others will need more time to study and think through the truths in the following books. Each chapter of <u>Finding the Way</u> is designed to develop a deeper relationship between the discipler and disciple. Your objective is to get to know Timothy and allow him to get to know and trust you, as well as allow Timothy to discover Biblical truths.

BOOK 1, CHAPTER 1: The Bible: Believe It or Not?

THE BIG IDEA

To discover Timothy's thinking and past experiences with the Bible and to invite Timothy to investigate the Bible as a resource for living.

KEY TEACHING POINTS

1. **The Bible is unique and unlike any other book in history.**
2. **The purpose of the Bible is threefold: for God to show Himself to people, to show people how they are to relate with others, and how they are to interact with God.**
3. **The fulfilled prophecies of the Bible lay a foundation for it's credibility.**

TEACHING OUTLINE

I. WHAT IS THE BIBLE?   PAGE 6
Published in more languages, and read by more people than any other
book, the Bible is actually a library of 66 books, written by 40 writers,
on 3 continents, over a period of 1500 years.

II. WHY WAS THE BIBLE WRITTEN?   PAGES 7-8
The Bible was written as a means for God to reveal Himself ; to set
forth principles and to give illustrations by which we can live, and
to show how we can have fellowship with God.

III. IS THE BIBLE CREDIBLE?   PAGES 9-10
The Bible is credible because the prophecies fulfilled through the life
of Christ are beyond chance.

IV. WHAT DOES THE BIBLE SAY ABOUT ITSELF?   PAGES 11-13
The Bible claims to be "God-breathed" (inspired), useful for teaching,
rebuke, correction and training in righteousness.

ADDITIONAL DISCUSSION QUESTIONS AND ILLUSTRATIONS

The following questions and illustrations may be helpful to stir your thinking.
For the greatest impact, use these as supplemental materials to your own personal
illustrations. A key to your success as a facilitator will be your ability
to ask open-ended questions to elicit response from Timothy.
Questions like...

> "...What does that mean to you?"
> "...Can you tell me more about that?"
> "...Why is that significant to you?"

Key questions will appear in purple type.

Off-the-Wall Answers

Diplomacy is critically important as you establish your relationship with Timothy. There
may be times when Timothy's answers or statements may cause you alarm. Perhaps the
best way to handle such a situation is simply to ask another question, rather than make
an attempt to refute the statement. Find common ground through the use of a personal
illustration and ending the story with, "I felt the same way at one time..." Keep in mind
that our goal is to create an environment in which Timothy will feel safe to open up.

Working Through the Lesson

Whether or not Timothy has completed the lesson, we suggest that you proceed through
the material, question by question, beginning with the "Warm Up" section.

Page 5

Question 3:

Q: "When your parents attended church, where did they attend?"

Q: "What has contributed to your current view of the Bible?"

Q: "On a scale of 1–10, how would you describe your familiarity with the Bible?"

Ask Timothy specifically about his parents' view of the Bible, church, God, and other questions to discover his spiritual background.

We suggest that you briefly share your own spiritual background, avoiding "preachy jargon," to facilitate Timothy's responsiveness.

Page 6

The Bible at a Glance chart (see page 15)

Q: "What is new or significant to you about how the Bible is organized?"

Q: "Have you studied any of the Bible as poetry in school? If so, what?"

Q: "Did you memorize the books of the Bible as a child?"

Remember to share your responses to these questions with Timothy in an effort to maintain a give-and-take relationship during your time together. Refer to the table of contents in your Bible and demonstrate how to find a given book, etc.

Three Purposes for the Bible

Page 7

THE PLUMBLINE
AN ILLUSTRATION

Professional wallpaper hangers constantly use a tool called a "plumbline" or "chalk-line" to ensure wallpaper is hung perfectly straight, up and down. (If you have a plumbline, you may want have it handy for visual impact) Amateurs, especially first-timers, sometimes fail to see the need for such effort. A friend recently wallpapered a bedroom for her child. Using her plumbline, she carefully hung the first sheet. However, as she progressed around the room, in an effort to conserve time and energy, she used the previous sheet as a guide. About half way through the job, she stepped back to view her work. It so happened that the paper had a distinctive stripe, which appeared to drift to the left after the second or third sheet — and decidedly so at the half way point. Her effort to save time had become a costly error.

The Bible refers to itself as a "plumbline." When we use it every day and line up our lives with what it says, we stay on course. When we don't, we run the risk of drifting, little by little at first, progressively further and further as we live our lives. In the end, ignoring the Bible's teachings will eventually put us far away from God's standards. That is why a daily visit to God's Word is so important.

Page 8

Daniel in the Lion's Den, Noah's Ark, and Jonah and the Whale are three of the most familiar stories in all of history.

Q: "As a child, do you remember what you thought when you heard these stories?"

Q: "Has their meaning changed for you as an adult? If so, how?"

Q: "How do these stories illustrate how God is involved in the lives of people today?"

A: **JONAH AND THE WHALE**
The importance of obeying God's directions
NOAH AND THE ARK
The holiness of God and His desire for man to live by His standards
DANIEL AND THE LION'S DEN
The protection available to God's people in tough times

Page 10

Pennies for your thoughts
Fulfilled prophecy regarding the life of Jesus goes way beyond "chance" as to his claim of being the Messiah.

Q: "What is your reaction to the ten pennies illustration?"

Q: "1000 to 1 are pretty long odds — how does this impact your understanding of Jesus? Why?"

Page 11

Filling in the Blanks
The answers are **(1) TEACHING (2) REBUKING (3) CORRECTING, AND (4) TRAINING IN RIGHTEOUSNESS.**

Q: "How do you handle correction… do you enjoy it? How do you react?"

Q: "In what way is God using the Bible in your life today?"
(For teaching, rebuking, etc.)

Pages 12-13

Questions regarding Luke 24:13-32

VERSE 19 Q: "How does the questioner refer to Jesus?"

VERSE 20 Q: "How did the religious hierarchy feel about it?"

VERSE 21 Q: "At this point, how much time had passed since Jesus' crucifixion?"

VERSE 22 Q: "Who were the first people to discover the empty tomb of Jesus?"

VERSE 23 Q: "What was the message they shared with the others?"

VERSE 24 Q: "Then what happened?"

VERSES 25-27 Q: "What source did Jesus cite to explain the recent events to His listeners?"

VERSES 28-32 Q: "Let's look at these verses carefully — what stands out on the human side?" (Look at His responses, think about His needs, review His choices, etc.)

Q: "Why do you think they did not at first recognize Jesus?"

Conclusion

Always make it a point to go over questions at the end of each chapter. The answers will reveal much about Timothy's learning curve and future needs. For additional study and reading, other materials are suggested at the bottom of the page. If you have copies of one or more of the books, and anticipate Timothy's need for further investigation, you may want to bring them with you to the session for the purpose of loaning them to Timothy.

How to Proceed

If Timothy does express the need for further study, explain that you would like to keep on course in Book 1, and that outside study may be necessary. Be sensitive. Many times questions may surface on contradictions, evolution, and other matters. For the most part, these are not the real issues of the heart. Continue in your efforts to invite Timothy to study the Bible for himself.

Two Classic Illustrations to Support the Existence of God

We have looked at what the Bible says about itself…but are there other evidences that support and give these claims credibility? The Bible says God created the heavens and the earth — but where is the evidence of His existence?

NOBODY MADE IT
A TRUE STORY

Sir Isaac Newton, famous for his discovery of the law of gravity, once had an atheist friend with whom he had many debates about the existence of God and the reliability of the Scriptures. Frustrated by his inability to communicate, Sir Isaac spent weeks on a project while his friend was out of town. Upon returning from his trip, Sir Isaac's friend visited him. As he entered the room, he was amazed to find an intricate wooden replica of the solar system, with all the planets to scale and with movable parts to show the movement of the planets in relationship to one another. The friend went on and on about the exquisite and precise detail and ingenuity of such a creation.

Finally, he asked Sir Isaac, "Who made such a marvelous model?" Sir Isaac replied, "Nobody made it, it just appeared."

"What?" the friend exclaimed. "Do you take me for a fool? Of course someone made it — stop joking with me and tell me who designed this elaborate, incredible replica of the universe!"

"Nobody made it. It simply appeared one day while you were away." The friend would not accept Sir Isaac's ludicrous explanation, and pressed him again and again to no avail. At last the friend grew angry and demanded, once and for all, a plausible explanation.

Sir Isaac replied: "You are so certain that someone had to have created this very poor imitation of the infinite universe, and yet you assert that the universe itself, a creation far more wondrous than this mere replica, just appeared, without a designer or a creator."

The design of the universe, as well as the scientific design specifications for life on the earth are two supporting evidences that what the Bible reveals about God's existence is true.

THE WATCHMAKER
AN ANALOGY

William Paley, an 18th century theologian and naturalist, used the following analogy as an apologetic argument for the existence of God. Paley argued that an earth without a Designer was like finding a watch in the woods. We would not automatically assume that the watch evolved from the rocks, leaves and dirt around it. Instead, we would assume that someone had first designed, then constructed the watch. Why? Because upon examination, we would see the intricate detail and craftsmanship evident in its makeup. Each part has a purpose. Each piece is an integral part of the whole, working with a hundred other pieces for the purpose of producing a means of accurately telling time. If one part is missing, the watch does not run. If one part is misshapen, the timepiece will not function as it is designed to function.

The earth was created to sustain life. It, like the watch, has a design.

Two hundred years after Paley first used his illustration, scientists began identifying precise design specifications without which the universe and the earth could not exist. To date, 32 critical design specifications for the earth and 24 for the universe have been identified. If any one of these specifications were altered or missing, the earth would not support life.

These discoveries show that the earth has a specific purpose (to provide life) and that the earth and the universe were precisely designed to achieve that purpose.

Adapted from *The Fingerprint of God, the Anthropic Principle* by astrophysicist Hugh Ross

Next Steps

1. *Set a day and time to get together again. Use page 4 in Timothy's material to record the date, day, time and place of your next meeting.*
2. *Assign Chapter Two: "Is God Relevant to My Life?" However, if you did not get through Chapter One, ask Timothy to review it and begin there next time. Proceed at a comfortable pace.*
3. *Make a note of any questions that you could not answer.*
4. *Make a copy of the diary page on pages 22 and 23 of this guide. Jot down what you have discovered about Timothy's life.*
5. *Pray for Timothy this week. A phone call, or a drop by visit from you would be an encouragement. When you call, ask about any concerns that were shared in this session.*
6. *Further reading and study: If Timothy has further questions or doubts regarding the credibility of the Bible, see suggested materials list at the bottom of page 14, Book 1.*

BOOK 1, CHAPTER 2: Is God Relevant to My Life?

THE BIG IDEA

To discover Timothy's view of God's relevance and to investigate whether God is involved personally in everyday life.

KEY TEACHING POINTS

1. **God is relevant to life as seen in His character and instructions to us about our work, relationships and money.**
2. **An initial understanding of who God is gives us a basis upon which we might trust Him.**

TEACHING OUTLINE

I. IS GOD RELEVANT TO MY LIFE?   **PAGES 19-24**
God is relevant because our work, relationships, money and
our needs matter to Him.

II. CAN I TRUST GOD WITH MY NEEDS?   **PAGES 25-27**
We are naturally skeptical because the world tends to say one
thing and do another, but God can be trusted because He says so,
and proves it daily. We can trust God with our lives.

ADDITIONAL DISCUSSION QUESTIONS AND ILLUSTRATIONS

As you begin, break the ice with questions about Timothy's week, family; share some of the highlights of your week as well. You may want to ask additional questions of Timothy to gain more insight into issues or personal matters. For example...

"...You mentioned last time that you did not grow up in a church, tell me what Sundays were like in your family."

Page 17

Warm Up Questions
Work through each question with Timothy. Remember, you are asking for Timothy's opinion in this section, not looking for a debate or argument. Remain open.

Take some time to discuss and ask additional questions regarding Timothy's view of God.
Q: "What do you feel has done most to shape your view of who God is? Why?"
Q: "Have there been recent events that have changed or altered your understanding in this area? If so, what?"

Share past or present circumstances and situations that have had an impact on your understanding. Give details on how these experiences are continuing to mold your view of God.

Q: "In your view, to what extent is God involved in everyday life and problems?"

Page 19

Principles from Colossians 3:23-25
First, allow time for Timothy to share answers and insights.
Then, highlight the following six principles from this passage of Scripture:

Page 20

1. We are to work wholeheartedly.
2. Our purpose is to please God, not men, in what we do.
3. God says He will reward us.
4. In reality, we are serving Christ.
5. Wrongdoing will be repaid.
6. God shows no favoritism.

Significant Relationships
Allow time for Timothy to share about the 5 significant relationships. Who are the most important people in Timothy's life? Why?

Page 21

Spend time discussing I Corinthians 13:4-7 (familiar verses to most people). The following questions may be helpful to guide the discussion:
Q: "Why are the ideals mentioned in the passage of Scripture so difficult for human beings to attain?" (The fact is, they are impossible without the help of God)
Q: "Can you think of anyone you know, or have read of, who has measured up to these high standards?" (Jesus Christ is the only one to do so)
Q: "What are we to do with these principles? How should they affect our behavior?"
Q: "Do you think it is possible for us to see these qualities in our lives? Why? How?"

Instructions for Marriage Partners

Discuss Timothy's marital situation. It may be helpful if you, as the leader, go first. Point out that God has guidelines and specific instructions in the Bible regarding all roles in the marriage and family…husbands, wives, children.

Page 22

READING ONE ANOTHER'S MAIL
AN ILLUSTRATION

The Bible is one place where reading your spouse's mail happens too often. Here, the Bible (actually a letter to a group of believers) gives instructions to the husband — simple and straight-forward directions to be read and applied by him to his life. However, many times the man reads the instructions God intends for the wife. All too often, the husband determines that his wife is evidently unaware of what the Bible says she is to do in a marriage relationship, and underlines the "good parts" for her. To be fair, the wife often does likewise. The results can be disastrous. The best way to handle Scripture passages like this is to take what is written to you and apply it. Let your spouse do the same. God will ultimately hold both accountable for the principles and instructions meant for them.

God and Your Wallet

Q: "Is money good, or bad?"

Q: "The Bible says, 'The love of money is the root of all evil,' what do you think that means?"

Page 23

Anxiety, Anger, Death and Hurt

Take time to read the verses out loud with Timothy. Suggest situations in your own life where these verses, or other similar verses, have been a help to you.

Page 24

Can I Trust God with My Needs (see page 67)

Note the list of 30 needs common to everyone.

Page 25

Self Worth Issues?

If you have picked up self worth issues in Timothy's life, share that Psalm 139 may be of help — perhaps even a passage of Scripture to commit to memory or spend time meditating on.

Page 26

God in pictures

Q: "What do these word pictures bring to mind as you read them?"

Page 27 Under the "Key" icon, review Timothy's responses. Again, here is where you will be able to ascertain whether or not Timothy is grasping the significance of the material. Answers here will give you a better feel for the pace you need to set. Take a few minutes to discuss the responses.

Next Steps:

1. *Record the date, time, and place of your next meeting on page 4 of Timothy's booklet.*
2. *If you sense it would not be an embarrassment, and if the location permits it, you may want to pray together before you leave. Ask about any particular challenge or need coming up this week.*
3. *If circumstances and schedules permit, try to do something fun together — sports, dinner, etc. Call Timothy during the week to say hello and to reconfirm your meeting.*
4. *Make notes in your diary to use as a prayer reminder for yourself.*
5. *Further reading and study: If Timothy has further questions or doubts regarding the lesson, see suggested materials list at the bottom of page 27, Book 1.*

BOOK 1, CHAPTER 3: Who Is Jesus?

THE BIG IDEA

To encourage Timothy to consider the evidence for Jesus' humanity as well as His deity.

KEY TEACHING POINTS

1. **Jesus entered time and space 2000 years ago as a man who walked, talked, ate, slept, got hungry, died on a cross, was buried, and rose again.**
2. **Jesus was more than a good man or a great teacher; He was God. His resurrection from the dead was one of many fulfilled prophecies that confirm His claims to deity.**

CHAPTER THREE

TEACHING OUTLINE

I. JESUS' HUMANITY   **PAGES 30-31**
Jesus experienced and understood suffering , temptation and
death so that we could relate to Him.

II. JESUS' DEITY   **PAGES 32-35**
Jesus was the promised Messiah.
Jesus' deity was revealed to His disciples.
Jesus' deity gave Him all authority and power to forgive sin and
raise people from the dead.
Jesus' deity was questioned initially by those who knew Him.

ADDITIONAL DISCUSSION QUESTIONS AND ILLUSTRATIONS

Be sure to cover all the Scriptures, either reading aloud or sharing how you both
answered the questions. Keep asking, "What does this mean to you?" or "What do
you hear in this verse?"

Read the quotes and ask for reactions. Discuss the Warm Up questions.
While on this page, refer to the quote on page 28.

Page 29

Hebrews 2:14
Q: "Have you ever feared death? If so, in what way?"
Q: "Do you have a fear of terminal illness? Growing old, or becoming
an invalid?"

Page 30

The box at the top right lists several names for Jesus. You will be studying
these later, but this would be a good time to ask…
Q: "What do you think is the significance of these names?"
Q: "What does it mean to you that Jesus experienced hunger, sadness, thirst,
fatigue — do you think He can sympathize with our weaknesses?"

Page 31

Key Scripture and question
Q: "Are you familiar with John the Baptist? Elijah? Jeremiah? Why would
people think Jesus was one of them?"

Page 32

Jesus said God revealed to Peter who He really was…
Q: "In your opinion, who was Jesus?"

Read Matthew 14: 22-33 aloud

Q: "What is happening as we pick up the story?"

Q: "Why do you think Jesus sought to be alone?"

Q: "Have you ever felt 'buffeted by the waves'? In what way?"

Page 33

Q: "Why do you think the disciples first reacted as they did?"

Q: Jesus said, "It is I." "In your opinion, why was this good news to them?"

Q: "At what point did Peter begin to sink?"

Q: "How might this story apply to our lives today?"

Note: Whatever Timothy's response to the last question on page 33, accept where he is, and continue to ask why he feels this way. This will give insight into Timothy's obstacles to belief and perhaps some hurts from the past. Invite him to continue investigating the Scriptures with you before drawing conclusions.

Spiritual background

Timothy may raise questions here about eternal life. Chapters 5 and 6 of this study deal with the subject in detail. The point here is the Jews' reaction

Page 34

to Jesus' claims of being the Messiah, i.e. if He were merely claiming to be a prophet or a great teacher they would not have had such a violent response.

Doubting Thomas

Q: "When you hear the term 'Doubting Thomas,' what comes to mind?"
(Believing Thomas would be a more descriptive phrase)

Page 35

Q: "What is Jesus' response to doubts? What do you think that says about our doubts?"

BECOMING AN ANT
ILLUSTRATION

If you had a great love for ants and wanted to communicate your love to them, what would be the best plan to accomplish it? You could feed them, provide them a better place to live, etc. — even try your best to learn and speak the "ant language." But to demonstrate your love, the best possible way would be to become an ant yourself so that you could identify with their struggles. This would require a tremendous sacrifice on your part as you gave up the benefits of human life to share the limitations that come with being an ant.

Timothy's View of Jesus

Be sensitive at this point. Chapters 4, 5, and 6 will go deeper into this issue. Timothy may be ready to receive Christ at this point. However, you may sense

Page 36

from the response and discussion that this is not the time. Don't push.

Philip Schaff Quote

Read the quote out loud and ask for Timothy's reactions to it.

Next Steps:

1. Assign next lesson, date, time and place.
2. Pray together, asking God to reveal Himself more and more to each of you as you continue your study.

BOOK 1, CHAPTER 4: Did Jesus Have A Purpose in Coming?

THE BIG IDEA

To allow Timothy to discover why Jesus came to earth, why and how He died and to establish the fact that He is coming again.

KEY TEACHING POINTS

1. Jesus came to provide the way for man to have a relationship with God.
2. Jesus did many miracles to demonstrate He was more than a mere man.
3. Jesus died on a cross by crucifixion, and He rose from the dead.
4. Jesus Christ will come again in the final days of the earth.

TEACHING OUTLINE

I. WHY DID JESUS CHRIST COME?   **PAGE 38**
Jesus came to earth to save us from our sins.
II. WHAT DID JESUS DO?   **PAGE 39**
Jesus led a life to be imitated, was the most influential teacher in history, offered hope to the outcasts of society, and demonstrated power over disease, nature and even death.
III. HOW DID JESUS DIE?   **PAGES 40-41**
He did not die because He had done anything wrong.
He knew in advance that He would be crucified, but He went to Jerusalem anyway.
He suffered and died to bring us peace with God.
He died for you.

IV. DID JESUS RISE AGAIN?   PAGES 42-43
Jesus' resurrection is a key to faith and was documented by
over 500 eyewitnesses, including all the disciples and later
the Apostle Paul.

V. WHAT ELSE IS LEFT FOR JESUS TO DO?   PAGE 44
The Bible says He will soon come again to take those who
believe with Him.

ADDITIONAL DISCUSSION QUESTIONS AND ILLUSTRATIONS

Zacchaeus
Ask Timothy if this story is a familiar one. If not, turn to Luke 19 and
read it together.

Page 38   **Q:** "What do you see in this story that tells us more about Jesus?"

Miracles
If Timothy is not familiar with most of the miracles, take time to read a few
together. If there is interest, note the references below for further study:

Page 39

Healing Miracles
   Lepers cleansed: Matthew 8:3; Luke 17:14
   Paralytic healed: Mark 2:3-12
   Nobleman's son: John 4:46-53
   Withered hand: Matthew 12:10-13
Nature Miracles
   Water to wine: John 2:6-10
   Quieted storm: Matthew 8:23-26; Matthew 14:32
   Huge fish catch: Luke 5:4-6; John 21:6
   Walk on water: Matthew 14:25-27
Death to Life Miracles
   Jairus' daughter: Matthew 9:18-26; Mark 5:22-43; Luke 8:41-56
   Widow's son: Luke 7:12-15
   Lazarus: John 11

Scripture references
   Zaccheus: Luke 19; Tax collector: Mark 2:14-17
   Samaritan woman: John 4
   Adulterous woman: John 8:3-11

Discussion questions

Q: Romans 5:8 "What is the difference between saying you love someone and proving it? What's the significance of Christ dying for us 'while we were still sinners'?"

Q: Isaiah 53:5,6 "In your opinion, how are we like the sheep mentioned in this passage? Why?"

Page 40

Vine's Expository Dictionary of Old and New Testament Words defines...

Transgressions: *Primarily a going aside, then, an overstepping of the prescribed limit*

Iniquity: *Lawlessness or wickedness or unrighteousness; "a condition of not being right, whether with God, according the standard of His holiness and righteousness, or with man, according to the standard of what man knows to be right by his conscience."*

Sin: *a missing of the mark (as in an archer aiming for the goal with his bow and missing the bulls-eye or even the whole board); wrongdoing.*

Justification
Justify: to acquit from guilt
Q: "What significance is there in the fact that Jesus was crucified between two thieves?"

Page 41

Doubts about the resurrection?
Don't attempt to answer all doubts and questions about the resurrection. Keep asking questions such as...

Page 42 **Q:** "How old were you when you first began to doubt? What did your parents believe? Are/Were there others in your life who influenced your view?"

Believing the Scriptures
Q: "When did the disciples believe the Scripture and the words that Jesus had spoken? Why do you think this is significant?"

Page 43

Encouraging Words
Paul tells us to "encourage each other with these words" in I Thessalonians 4:15-18. Discuss why these words should be comforting to us today...

Page 44

Three final items in God's plan: (1) Jesus is coming soon (2) He is bringing His reward with Him (3) He will give to everyone according to what he has done.

Final thoughts
Take time to talk through what impressed you both from this study. Don't attempt to convince, debate, or persuade at this point. Encourage Timothy to spend time reviewing the Scriptures, thinking and praying about their significance in his/her life.

Page 45

Next Steps

1. *Assign next chapter and write down date, time, place.*
2. *Pray together.*
3. *Contact Timothy during the week.*
4. *Fill in your diary.*

BOOK 1, CHAPTER 5: Can God Accept Me?

THE BIG IDEA

To help Timothy understand that God truly accepts us and desires a relationship with us because He is able to meet the deepest needs in our lives.

KEY TEACHING POINTS

1. We all have needs in our lives. We can't survive alone. Our needs are physical, emotional, and spiritual.
2. A look at God's character displays His desire to meet our needs.
3. Jesus Christ is the only answer to meet our spiritual needs.

TEACHING OUTLINE

I. WHAT ARE MY NEEDS?   **PAGES 48–51**
God meets our human need for acceptance, approval, attention and comfort,but His greatest work is in the area of meeting our spiritual need, which only He can do.

II. WHY WOULD GOD WANT TO MEET THESE NEEDS?   **PAGE 52**
Because of His loving character, God continually is reaching out to us to meet our needs.

CHAPTER FIVE

III. HOW DOES GOD MEET THESE NEEDS?   **PAGES 53-55**

Even though we are undeserving and selfish at heart, God sent Jesus Christ to provide a way for us to live, now and eternally, with Him.

ADDITIONAL DISCUSSION QUESTIONS AND ILLUSTRATIONS

Read through the Warm Up questions taking as much time as Timothy needs. Then, to set up the lesson, share about a time in your life when you felt lonely or empty and how family and friends did, or did not, respond to your needs. Timothy may share similar experiences, and volunteer them at this point.

See Chart page 67

Q: "What are your top three needs?"

Page 48 Share your top three with Timothy. Discuss the definitions of the ones you named.

Met and Unmet Childhood Needs (Optional Exercise):

Spend time discussing how these needs were met or unmet in your childhood. If there was a need for acceptance, was it met by your mother or father? — if by Mom, put a check by that need, if by Dad, an X. Draw a zero next to those needs that were not met by either parent. Talk through the significance.

See page 19 "Bellhop or Landlord"
Compare and contrast those perceptions of God with the characteristics revealed here.

Page 52

After answering the questions on John 3:16-17, ask...
Q: "Why is it significant that the Bible says Jesus did not come to condemn the world?"

Page 53 **Q:** "What words are used in Roman 5:6-8 to describe us?" (powerless, ungodly, sinner) "Do you think these are accurate? Why? Why not?"

Discuss the first two questions thoroughly.
Define your terms: Talk through the way the terms Justice, Mercy, and Grace can be applied to your lives. Share some examples from your life.

Page 54

John 5:24
The two responses God wants from us: hear and believe. The three things He has promised: eternal life, no condemnation, death to life. (These concepts will be explained more fully in the next lesson)

Reflections
Q: "About what are you wearied or burdened?" (Spend some time praying about these matters with Timothy, specifically asking Christ to give rest)

Page 56

Next Steps:

1. *Set date, time and place for next session.*
2. *Assign chapter 6.*
3. *Pray together for individual and mutual needs.*
4. *Record insights in your diary.*
5. *Further Reading and Study: If Timothy continues to struggle with the issue of God's character, further reading is suggested on page 55.*

BOOK 1, CHAPTER 6: How Can I Be Forgiven?

THE BIG IDEA

To allow Timothy to discover how to be forgiven, and gain a relationship with God without forcing a decision on the spot.

KEY TEACHING POINTS

1. **No one is perfect. Everyone has sinned and is separated from God. Therefore, every person has a need to be forgiven.**
2. **The basis for receiving forgiveness is not on the evidence of our good works or activities, but Jesus Christ's substitution for us on the cross.**
3. **Forgiveness is a gift and must be received. One of the results is we also have eternal life with God which begins in the present.**

TEACHING OUTLINE

ADDITIONAL DISCUSSION QUESTIONS AND ILLUSTRATIONS

Open by reading and discussing the quote on page 57 by political philosopher,
Hannah Arendt. Then, work through the Warm Up section, sharing answers.

Page 58

Definition of Forgiveness
<u>Vine's Dictionary of Old and New Testament Words</u> gives the following
definition…

Forgive: *to send forth, to send away, denoting a dismissal, a release of debts
or sins, as being completely canceled.*

Page 59

Is man really a "sinner"? If Timothy feels man is basically good, not sinful,
ask why.

If Timothy offers objections to man being a sinner (expressing that man is
basically good), don't argue. Listen and repeat what is said, then suggest
that you continue investigating what the Bible has to say and go on to the
next Scripture.

**Pages
59-60**

Romans 2:1
Q: "Are there examples in your life where you judge others for words or
actions that you are guilty of yourself? Explain."

Discuss the diagram at the bottom of page 60. Review the Scriptures on the
previous page if necessary.

Page 61

Discuss the sensitive subject of good works with Timothy. Use this to lead into the diagram at the bottom of the page — "We try to do the right things to get to God..."

Page 62

Titus 3:5 says "He saves us not because of the righteous things we have done, but because of His mercy."

Q: "What does this say about what God is providing for us? What does this mean to you personally?"

Page 64

How to receive forgiveness
I John 1:7-9 offers us a benefit or reward: "If we walk in the light...we will have fellowship with one another..."

It goes on to say: "*If we claim to be without sin*, we deceive ourselves and *the truth is not in us.*"

"*If we confess our sins*, he is faithful and just and will *forgive us our sins and purify us from all unrighteousness.*"

Ephesians 2:8,9
Q: "Why does the Bible say God won't accept our works as a payment for sin?"

RECEIVING A GIFT
AN ILLUSTRATION

Let's say I were going to give you this pen as a gift. My part is to offer it to you. What is your part? You must receive it. Only then is it actually in your possession. (Go through the motions as you share)

Page 64

Ask Timothy to read from his/her response on how to receive God's forgiveness. Be discerning at this point. Ask if there is a desire to receive God's love and forgiveness. If there is resistance, move on. If there is willingness, say something like: "Let's pray together. Remember, God is not as interested in your words as He is in the attitude of your heart..." If Timothy is unsure how to pray, offer your help by praying a phrase at a time, asking Timothy to follow.

"*I know I am a sinner, I need a Savior. I ask Christ to come in and take total control of my life.*"

CHAPTER SIX

Cross diagram page 62

Page 65 Turn back and write the words "hear and believe" from John 5:24 above the cross in the diagram. Then write the three results of this choice "eternal life, no condemnation, from death to life" under the tree and the word "God."

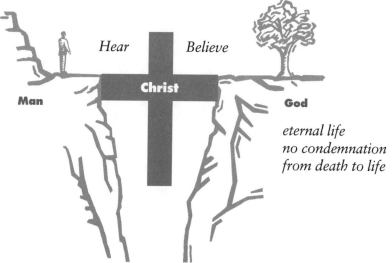

Hear *Believe*

Man Christ **God**

eternal life
no condemnation
from death to life

Next Steps:

1. *Pray together.*
2. *Give Timothy Book 2 and assign chapter 1. Write down day, date and time.*
3. *Open Book 2 and go over the table of contents. Timothy will need a Bible for this study, and there is a memory verse for each chapter. Turn to page 10 and point out the section on Scripture memory. You may want to read through this section to prepare Timothy for your next session.*
4. *As the leader, you need to know if Timothy has a Bible. If not, suggest that an NIV (New International Version) would be best because the study is based on it. You may want to provide an inexpensive paperback NIV, or offer to go to a bookstore and help pick out a Bible.*

   Point out the Scripture memory verse on page 10 and the perforated cards at the end of the book. Share a brief "faith story" of how memorizing Scripture has helped you in your Christian life.

B O O K   T W O

Knowing the Truth

INTRODUCTION TO BOOK 2

The Bible is our source and standard for truth. "Thy word is truth" (Jn. 17:17).
Applied truth provides a foundation for our values and a guide for our daily lives.
Knowing the Truth digs deeper into God's Word and lays a strong Biblical foundation
for a person's Christian walk. Eternal assurance, the Holy Spirit, Satan, temptation,
insidership and personal testimony preparation are the subjects of Book 2. Timothy
also begins to memorize specific Scripture verses that correlate with each lesson.
The Scripture texts are not printed, and so Timothy will need his own Bible. You
will want to help him select one and learn how to use it.

BOOK 2, CHAPTER 1: Gaining Eternal Assurances

THE BIG IDEA

To demonstrate that every believer can know for certain
they have eternal life and begin to enjoy the benefits
of that life today.

KEY TEACHING POINTS

1. Jesus Christ is the only way to eternal life. All we can
do is surrender our lives to His control and accept His
free gift of salvation resulting in eternal life.

2. We are assured of eternal life because of what the
Bible says and the inward reassurance of God's Spirit
that we are God's children.

3. God's Spirit comes to live within us when we receive Christ. This is evidenced by an ongoing change of attitudes, actions, convictions and encouragement.

4. Eternal life begins now (not in heaven someday in the future).

TEACHING OUTLINE

MEMORY VERSE:

The importance of Scripture memorization is introduced on pages 10 and 11. Memorize I John 5:11-13.

ADDITIONAL DISCUSSION QUESTIONS AND ILLUSTRATIONS

Open with the Warm Up section and the excerpt from Indiana Jones' adventure as he had in his possession the precious jewel, only to lose his grasp and see it slip into the quicksand — lost forever.

Some people think our salvation can slip through our fingers. What does the Bible say?

CHAPTER ONE

Page 4

Preparation for the Leader
If Timothy has not prepared for the lesson ahead of time, take a few moments to discuss and discern the situation: Lack of time? Difficulty locating the books of the Bible? Be sensitive to the fact that it may take a while for Timothy to become adept at locating Scripture references.

You may want to work through the lesson together, looking up verses, filling in blanks, etc. Another approach would be to take a week and review the chart of "The Bible at a Glance" on Page 15 of Book 1, *Finding the Way*. Have Timothy turn to each book in the Bible, pointing out how they are arranged by chapters and verses. Direct attention to the Table of Contents and the page numbers listed for each book. Spend some time reviewing other features such as: maps, margin notes, concordances, etc. This would be an excellent opportunity to challenge Timothy to memorize the books of the Bible — adding that it would enhance study in the weeks and years to come. Use your discretion.

Page 5

Vine's definition...
Repentance: *Literally, to perceive afterwards, signifying a change of one's mind or purpose, always in the New Testament involving a change for the better, an amendment, and always of...repentance from sin, and this change of mind involves both a turning from sin and a turning to God.* The parable of the prodigal son is an outstanding illustration of this. Christ began His ministry with a call to repentance (Matt. 4:17)...the call is addressed to the individual.

LEAVE THE DRIVING TO US
AN ILLUSTRATION

This illustrates Christ's desire to be Lord and Master, not just Savior. He wants the control of our lives, to direct and guide us for our good and His glory. In order to do this, we must surrender the control of our lives to Him. Discuss with Timothy the meaning of the word "surrender" and why it is a good term to describe what is necessary if we are to experience intimacy with God. Share illustrations from your own life of admitting you were completely powerless and turning your will and life over to God, including when you first received Christ, as well as other times and areas of life that you have surrendered to God. Someone once referred to this kind of surrender as "coming out of the cave with your hands up."

Page 6

A New Creation

Discuss what becoming a new creation, as described in 2 Corinthians 5:17 means. If Timothy is a fairly new Christian, and is struggling with habits and some areas of his/her life that do not seem to fit this description of being new, explain the "process" of God's conforming us to His image. God's Spirit within us makes us a "new creation", but God continues to conform us into His image little by little, day by day. Spiritual growth is a process similar to physical growth, developing through stages of infancy, childhood, adolescence, to adulthood. (The video teaching series Living Proof II deals with this issue of "what changes and what doesn't" when we receive Christ.)

Concentrate on the questions in the lesson in the following pages of Chapter One. Continue to ask for the "the story behind the story" of Timothy's answers, ask questions about the questions and the Scriptures in order to draw Timothy's attention to what God is saying in these verses.

> Continue to ask for the "story behind the story" of Timothy's answers.

Page 7

Q: "What comes to your mind when the term "eternal life" is used? What does that mean to you personally?"

Page 8

Q: "In what way(s) have you experienced the kind of life Jesus is talking about in John 10:10? With what do you struggle that keeps you from experiencing the abundant life?"

Read "Hooked on a Feeling" together —
Q: "What are your feelings: antagonistic, receptive, skeptical, hungry, puzzled?"
Q: "Is there something from your background or previous experience that you are having difficulty overcoming?"

If Timothy has been taught that a person can lose his salvation, this lesson may be difficult. Questions may surface regarding certain Scripture references. Be aware that even if there is acceptance of the assurance of eternal life, there still may be times in which Timothy struggles emotionally with this issue. Be patient. Don't try to debate and persuade.

Note: If Timothy has suffered abandonment from a parent or close family member, he/she may grapple with the feeling that God could also abandon him. Encourage Timothy to memorize I John 5:11-13 and meditate on it often.

Scripture Memory Verse
Don't skip this section. Even if you personally have difficulty memorizing Scripture, ask God to help you in the process as you help Timothy. Remember: you must memorize if you expect Timothy to. It's critical for growth. Every person who has devoted the time and effort to this one discipline says that nothing else benefits them as greatly. Peace, lifestyle changes, reassurance, joy, character development — these are but a few of the rewards of memorizing and meditating on Scripture.

Cover pages 10 and 11 thoroughly with Timothy. Share your own experiences, good and bad.

Next Steps:

1. *Review I John 5:11-13. Encourage Timothy to go over this verse daily as he begins to memorize Galatians 5:22,23.*
2. *Assign chapter 2 — point out the memory verse card in the back of the book. Write down date, time and place for the next session.*
3. *Pray together.*

BOOK TWO

BOOK 2, CHAPTER 2: Discovering the Holy Spirit

THE BIG IDEA

For Timothy to gain a solid foundation of understanding the Person and work of the Holy Spirit.

KEY TEACHING POINTS

1. **The Holy Spirit is God. God is expressed in three Persons: Father, Son and Holy Spirit.**
2. **Every believer has the indwelling Holy Spirit.**
3. **The functions of the Holy Spirit are multi-faceted, including convicting us of sin, giving us power to abstain from sin and live a holy life, and giving us spiritual gifts.**
4. **Every believer who is living a life yielded to the Holy Spirit and led by Him will evidence the fruit of love, joy, peace, etc.**

TEACHING OUTLINE

I. WHO IS THE HOLY SPIRIT?   **PAGES 14–15**
The Holy Spirit is a Person.

II. WHO HAS THE HOLY SPIRIT?   **PAGES 15–16**
Every believer possesses the Holy Spirit.

III. WHAT DOES THE HOLY SPIRIT DO?   **PAGES 17–18**
The Holy Spirit provides inward encouragement, conviction
and power as well as outward spiritual gifts.

IV. HOW DOES ONE LIVE AND WORK WITH THE HOLY SPIRIT?   **PAGES 19–21**
Our new inward motivation produces what the
Bible calls "Fruit."

MEMORY VERSE
Memorize Galatians 5:22,23.

ADDITIONAL DISCUSSION QUESTIONS AND ILLUSTRATIONS

Begin with a review of I John 5:11-13 and ask Timothy to recite Galatians 5:22,23 from memory. Talk about what these verses mean.

Ask Timothy to share his/her understanding of the Person of the Holy Spirit. Take time to discover how Timothy came to this belief. Is it a result of past teaching? Family influence? Other?

**Pages
13-14**

Some will challenge the use of the term *Trinity*, arguing it is not a Biblical word. Most cults refute this concept. Encourage openness and continued exploration of what the Bible teaches on the subject. Following is a partial list of Scriptural references supporting this doctrine:

Matthew 3:16; Matthew 28:19; Romans 8:9; I Corinthians 12:3-6;
II Corinthians 13:14; Ephesians 4:4-6; I Peter 1:2; Jude 20,21;
Revelation 1:4,5.

There are many other Scriptures which ascribe the same eternal qualities to each of the three persons of the Trinity. The principle of logic says if A=B and A=C, then B=C. Other passages reveal that each person in the Trinity is described as eternal, holy, true, omnipresent, omnipotent, omniscient, the Creator, the Sanctifier, the Author of all spiritual operations, the Source of eternal life, Teacher, raising Christ from the dead, inspiring the prophets and supplying ministers to the Church.

Three in one illustrations

Emphasize that any earthly or human analogy to the Trinity falls short of completely describing the mystery and the full scope of this truth. The illustrations of the man and egg are only to give us some insight.

Page 14

I Thessalonians 5:19 in the NIV translations reads: "Do not put out the Spirit's fire." In other translations it reads: "Do not quench the Spirit" and the idea of quenching a fire is implied. The names for the Holy Spirit might vary from one translation to the next. Clarify this with your Timothy if there seems to be confusion.

Page 15

When you discuss the questions and answers you will note that many are open-ended, inviting continued study. You may find that Timothy does not grasp the content of some passages. Gently share your answers for clarification when this seems to be the case. New Christians or seekers often write their opinion when the question is asking, "What does this verse say?" Other questions will ask for an opinion only. Take care not to squash Timothy's curiosity or willingness to be vulnerable and honest.

Members Only

This section may present difficulties for Timothy. Draw attention to what the verses actually say. Be honest: if this teaching is hard for you personally, say so. It is natural for us to want to understand a truth before accepting or surrendering to it. The point is, we do not have to "like" the truth, but we must accept and surrender to Him.

Page 16

Spiritual Gifts

If Timothy has not heard of spiritual gifts, or has a background in which certain gifts were emphasized to the exclusion of others, you might want to spend some time looking up the Scriptures listed beside each.

Page 18

Getting Your House in Order

Romans 6:11-14. Describe some of the good activities this passage might indicate for your life.

Page 19

My Heart, Christ's Home is an excellent little booklet that compares our hearts to a physical house. It is a good resource for depicting our bodies as homes for the Holy Spirit. It is inexpensive and would make a great gift for your Timothy.

Bad habits

If Timothy is a Christian, determine if there is an on-going battle with any acts or habits. Be careful. Some areas may require the help of a professional, such as a pastor, counselor, etc. However, your availability as an interested listener could be a beginning and will minister at this point.

Page 20

A. Z. Tozer quote

Close the session by reading the quote on page 22 and sharing any temptations against moral purity that may be presenting themselves from TV, movies, co-workers, etc.

Page 22

Next Steps:

1. *Pray together.*
2. *Assign chapter 3 and memory verse.*
3. *Write down day, date and time of next meeting.*
4. *Call Timothy this week and ask specifically about temptations.*
5. *Update diary.*

BOOK 2, CHAPTER 3: Knowing Your Enemy

THE BIG IDEA

To forewarn and forearm Timothy with the knowledge that our enemy, Satan, is alive and well and desires to shipwreck our lives.

KEY TEACHING POINTS

1. **Satan is real and described in the Bible in many ways. We dare not take him lightly.**
2. **Satan was once an angel and desired to usurp God's authority and become like Him. He will not succeed.**
3. **Satan and his forces are extremely clever, subtle and very powerful. He deceived Eve and attempted to snare Christ.**
4. **God has not left us defenseless. Although Satan is more powerful than any human being, he is a defeated foe because of what Christ did on the cross. We will fight daily battles with him, but the final victory is assured. Christ arms us with the Word, prayer and the Holy Spirit.**

TEACHING OUTLINE

 ## MEMORY VERSE:
Memorize I Peter 5:8,9.

ADDITIONAL DISCUSSION QUESTIONS AND ILLUSTRATIONS

Begin by reviewing the memory verse, I Peter 5:8,9, then review the two previous verses.

Q: "Which of these descriptions of Satan is new to you? How do these add
to your understanding of Satan?"

Page 24   Note: Timothy may have questions about the context and understanding
of these passages, If so, answer briefly from your own understanding, but
don't get sidetracked from continuing in the lesson. Many questions will
be answered as you continue through the study.

Satan's five "I wills" from Isaiah 14:12-15
    I will ascend to heaven.
    I will raise my throne above the stars of God.
Page 25   *I will sit enthroned on the mount of assembly.*
    I will ascend above the tops of the clouds.
    I will make myself like the Most High.
Q: "What kind of a person says these kinds of things?"

BOOK TWO

"Devil of a Time"

Read the quote together. Timothy may verbalize doubts about the kind of God that would allow suffering that results from the presence and power of Satan in the earth. Depending upon Timothy's receptivity, you may want to share verse on God's sovereignty as well as His goodness.

Page 25

Case Study A: Adam and Eve

Read Genesis 3:1-5 together. Work through the following questions:

Q: "What is the progression of the temptation?" (Eve saw, she took, she ate, then gave to her husband)

Page 26

Q: "What did she observe about the fruit?" (It was good for food, pleasing to the eye, desirable for gaining wisdom)

Q: "What did they do once they realized they were naked?" (Covered themselves)

Q: "How did they react when God was walking in the garden?" (They were afraid)

Q: "How did God respond?" (He asked two questions)

Q: "How did Adam respond?" (Blamed others)

Discuss with Timothy the basic principles regarding temptation that are revealed in this passage: Satan appeals to our senses and casts doubt on God's Word and character. Temptation is progressive: see, take, do, cover-up, blame others.

Q: "Have you seen this progression at work in your life?"

Scripture vs. Temptation

The question at the top of page 27 emphasizes the fact that Jesus quoted Scripture every time to refute Satan. Discuss how Jesus might have spent time in Hebrew school memorizing Scripture, hiding it in His heart.

Page 27

Make a point to apply this truth to the importance of Timothy's Scripture memorization efforts.

Spiritual Armor —

Make sure Timothy has identified all of the various parts of the armor of God.

Q: "Why is it important for you and me to take advantage of the 'full armor' of God?"

Q: "According to this passage, why do we need to?"

If Timothy expresses misgivings about his ability to pray effectively, refer to Romans 8:26,27: "In the same way, the Spirit helps us in our weakness. We do not know what we ought to pray for, but the Spirit himself intercedes for us with groans that words cannot express. And he who searches our hearts knows the mind of the Spirit, because the Spirit intercedes for the saints in accordance with God's will."

Page 28

Getting Offensive

Q: "What does James 4:7 say about the devil?"

I John 2:3,4 says that the indication of our submission to God is if we obey His commands.

Scouting Report

Be a specific as you can be in your own answers, and encourage Timothy to be specific, too. For example, "I struggle with lust" is general as opposed to, "I will be traveling out of town this week. The X-rated movies available in the motels are a big temptation. I will commit not to watch these, and choose some healthy activities instead, such as reading a good book, spending some time in the Word and prayer, calling friends in that city who are growing Christians. If I feel overwhelmed with temptation, I will call my Timothy leader, my wife or friend and share my struggle and feelings and ask for prayer.

Next Steps:

1. *Pray together about concerns and temptations.*
2. *Ask if there is anything else that needs to be discussed or shared.*
3. *Assign chapter 4 and the memory verse. Write down the day, date, and time for the next meeting.*
4. *Update diary.*

BOOK 2, CHAPTER 4: Dealing with Temptation

THE BIG IDEA

> **To teach Timothy the basis of a life of obedience and what we are to do if we stray from the path.**

KEY TEACHING POINTS

> **1. At the heart of our obedience is God's love for us and our love for Him.**
> **2. Everyone will be tempted in this life, and everyone will fail.**
> **3. When we fail, God has provided a means of forgiveness through Christ. Our relationship with God is not severed, but our fellowship may be. Confession restores our fellowship.**

4. Ongoing obedience is a process that is made possible through our knowledge of God's Word and His Spirit's enabling; we cannot do it on our own.

TEACHING OUTLINE

MEMORY VERSE:
Memorize I Corinthians 10:13.

ADDITIONAL DISCUSSION QUESTIONS AND ILLUSTRATIONS

This lesson picks up the theme of temptation inherent in the previous chapter dealing with Satan. Begin by reviewing the Scripture memory verse: this time, you go first.

Q: "What three assurances regarding temptation are given in
I Corinthians 10:13?"
Cover each question and Scripture carefully. The implied message here is that we will all fail — but we are not lost — we can find the path of obedience once again.

**Pages
32-33**

Refer to the quote in the circle "Been there, done that" and the fact that Jesus understands our temptation and will provide the strength to resist.

Confessing Christians
Timothy will probably name you as one person with whom sharing is possible. If you are the only one, it may indicate that close relationships may be a problem. Encourage Timothy to develop friendships, attend church, CBMC prayer breakfasts, small group Bible studies, etc, to develop deeper relationships.

Page 34

Describe in your own words the illustration of 2 Timothy 3:16, then ask…
Q: "How have you seen it at work in your life?"

Diagram
Use an example from your own life to walk through the four steps. Without taking too much time, illustrate how God used your family, friends, and others as a means of support, rebuke, correction. Tell how you got back on the path and what you learned in the process.

Spend time in Romans 6:12-14 and the surrounding verses. If Timothy does not know how to answer the last question about areas in his life, share your answers then work through it together.

Page 35

Don't get sidetracked
There may be a tendency to spend more time on the first question dealing with God's will at the expense of the second which deals with obedience. There will be an entire study on God's will in Book 3.

Page 36

> There is always tension regarding friends and companions. On the one hand, we encourage Timothy to stay in contact with "lost friends" while at the same time we encourage fellowship with "wise" Christians. However, here the emphasis is on "wise counsel."

After covering the questions on John 14:21, keep reading verses 23 and 24, then ask,

Page 37 **Q:** "What comes first: Obedience or love?"
(It is not a matter of either/or, rather both/and)

Love results in obedience; obedience demonstrates love is genuine.

Q: "Is the motivation for obedience a matter of *must* or *will?*
I must obey, or I will obey? Why?"

When the Holy Spirit comes, He gives new willingness and love for God that results in "I will" rather than "I must." Duty and obligation are only good for the short-term, while love and willingness are long-term motivators.

Page 38

Hebrews 12: 1-13 may be painful for someone from an abusive background. Remind Timothy this refers to a good father and appropriate discipline, not abuse.

B O O K   T W O

Next Steps:

1. *Pray together about a specific temptation.*
2. *Call Timothy during the week.*
3. *Assign the next chapter, write down the day, date and time.*
4. *Update the diary.*

BOOK 2, CHAPTER 5: Your Calling as an Insider

THE BIG IDEA

To ensure that Timothy understands God brings us into a relationship with Him, not just for our benefit alone, but that we might bring others to Him as a result — our family, friends, neighbors and work relationships are the unique and primary mission field in which God has placed us, and to which God has called us.

KEY TEACHING POINTS

1. An "insider" is "in the world" and therefore can relate to searching people in areas of personal influence without being "too preachy," while at the same time not embracing values and behaviors that are "of the world."
2. To be effective, an "insider" must have "common ground" with non-believers.
3. We are more effective if we work as a team with other believers.
4. Busyness and over-commitment will render us ineffective as an insider.

TEACHING OUTLINE

I.   WHAT IS AN INSIDER?   **PAGES 42-43**
To be an effective influence on our culture we must live "in" society without becoming influenced by society — it is the principle of "common ground.'

II. HOW CAN I BE AN INSIDER?   **PAGE 44**
God has us positioned right were He wants us. Our role is to prepare for the battle, not run from it.

III. HOW CAN I SURVIVE AS AN INSIDER?   PAGES 45-46
The reality of Christ within us, combined with the fellowship of
the Christian community, sustains us. Our use of time and
resources give us margin for ministry.

IV. WHAT IS AN INSIDER'S VISION?   PAGES 47-49
To be effective an insider must envision his or her role as an
integral part of a great army whose mission is to help fulfill the
Great Commission.

 ## MEMORY VERSE:
Memorize I Corinthians 7:24 and review with Timothy.

ADDITIONAL DISCUSSION QUESTIONS
AND ILLUSTRATIONS

As you prepare for your time with Timothy, read Chapter 2 of Jim Petersen's
Lifestyle Discipleship. Petersen's insights regarding the concept of "insiders"
will prove helpful. Another book that deals with the reality of the time crunch
and over-commitment is Dr. Richard Swensen's, *Margin*.

Begin by reviewing I Corinthians 7:24 as well as the four previous memory verses.

 Inside Quotes
Read aloud the quotes by Jim Petersen and Charles Swindoll regarding
serving as insiders in an unbelieving world.

Page 41   **Q:** "Why do you think serving on the inside is difficult for most people?
What factors tend to pull us away?"

Warm Up
Q: "Does this concept challenge any beliefs or teachings that you have
embraced in the past? How so?"
Jesus prayed that we would be "in" the world, not of it; yet elsewhere we
read that we are to be separate and "come out from among them."
Discuss the distinctions between the two.

 Paul describes his "insidership" in I Corinthians 9:19-23. Discuss what
it would be like if we really personalized this passage. How would our
lives change?

Page 42

Many of Timothy's questions will be answered as you move through the study. This would be a good time to encourage Timothy to begin thinking about being a part of a Living Proof I small group study. If you have been a part of such a group, share the benefits.

Page 43

Common Ground

The list is meant to challenge our "comfort zones." There may be some areas we need to rethink; others that are obviously not appropriate. However, Timothy may be still young enough in the faith as to be unaware of stumbling-blocks for others. Work through the list, discussing various concerns.

Read I Peter 2:12 aloud. Verse 11 says we are to abstain from sinful desires, while the remainder of the passage speaks to what we should do. Here is the balance of being "in" and not "of" the world. If Timothy is using this "insider" concept as an excuse to indulge sinful habits, discuss these verses and the implications.

Page 44

Outside Reading

If Timothy is a reader or needs more challenge, assign this exercise: Make a list of the authors and books listed thus far in Operation Timothy and begin reading through each of them. This would be a good time to share some of the books that have made the greatest impact on your own life.

Page 46

Meditating on John 15

The entire fifteenth chapter of John can be used as an exercise in meditation, especially for the power source of all of Christian living and specifically for the issues of insidership and margin. Spend some time meditating on the analogy of the vine and branches. If you have time, read through the chapter and discuss your insights.

Page 47

Quality and Quantity

Work through the list of people Timothy has included on the chart "I Am An Insider." Focus on the kind of time being spent with each: quality and quantity. Determine if there are areas that are out of balance; if so, point out the possibility to Timothy. Discuss opportunities and possible hurdles for building closer relationships.

Page 48

Q's: "How are you doing in giving these people quality time and quantity time? Are there people listed (or not listed) with whom you want to develop a closer relationship? What are the hurdles? What would you have to change in order to have the time? Do you have relationships with lost people?"

Page 49

Running on Empty?
Carefully ask questions about the various areas of Timothy's life and adjust the "gauges" if necessary. Make a point to share any struggles that you are having and how you are trying to adjust your time commitments to resolve them.

Next Steps:

1. *Pray together.*
2. *Assign next chapter, set date, time and place for your next session.*
3. *Update diary.*

BOOK 2, CHAPTER 6: Telling Others About Christ

BOOK TWO

THE BIG IDEA

To become more effective as a witness for Christ, we will clarify our message (the hope of Christ) and how we came to know Him — with specific help enabling Timothy to write out that unique story.

KEY TEACHING POINTS

1. **God has called all believers to share their faith — there are no exceptions.**
2. **The message is clear and simple: Christ, as God, became a man who lived, died and rose again to forgive our sins. Only as we receive this gift of a relationship with Christ will we experience forgiveness and have eternal life — now and forever.**
3. **Every Christian has a story to tell: my life without Christ, how I came to know Him personally, my changed and changing life with Christ.**

TEACHING OUTLINE

I. WHY SHOULD I TELL OTHERS?   **PAGE 52**
Although some may be hesitant to do so at first, Jesus has commanded us to share our faith.

MEMORY VERSE:

Memorize I Peter 3:15,16 and review with Timothy.

ADDITIONAL DISCUSSION QUESTIONS AND ILLUSTRATIONS

This is a lengthy lesson. Take as many weeks as you need to work through it thoroughly.
Begin with a review of the current memory verse, then work through the previous verses.

Obstacles
Q: "What seems to be getting in the way as you attempt to share your faith
with others?" (Discuss similar or other problems you are facing personally
Page 52   in this area)

Effective Communication
Discuss the importance gentleness and respect play in effective communication.
Give examples of how we sometimes come across in a condescending or harsh
Page 53   manner, if we are not careful.

Read through Acts 1:8, John 3:16, and I Corinthians 15:1-6 underscoring the
essential points. This lesson assumes that Timothy is or has become a Christian.
However, many people have stated that it was only when they started to write
out their testimony that they fully understood the gospel and accepted Christ.
Be sensitive to this fact.

Raising the Flag
Brainstorm together and jot down as many one-sentence flag-raisers as you
can in five minutes. Record them on page 64.
Page 54

Faith Stories

Work through events in your lives that would classify as "Faith Stories" and take time to write one out on page 64. Use an outline form, do not include details.

Diagram

Work through the diagram and point out the progression, noting how the sharing tools fit with the cultivation process.

Living Proof

Again encourage Timothy to pray about going through a Living Proof I video study group. You, as a leader, might consider starting one, inviting Timothy and your spouses to be a part of it, along with several other couples.

The *Living Proof* I & II drama is gripping and relates to the common struggles with which we all deal in growing and sharing our faith with others. The series is designed to be flexible, allowing you to meet once a week, twice a month, or even once a month. It can be used in a Sunday School format, taking two sessions per Sunday.

Read through Acts 26 together, making note of key principles that surface in the passage.

Writing Timothy's Testimony

Don't be surprised if Timothy has not completed this section. This is a long session. You may want to pick up here next time.

Pages 56-63

You may notice some reluctance on Timothy's part. Satan would love to cause confusion and bring up doubts. Simply work through any unfinished portions, discussing and filling in the appropriate blanks as you do. You can refine the material later — just get it down now.

If Timothy has completed the testimony section, have him/her read it out loud to you. Repeat back some of the essential points and give plenty of praise. Share what made an impact on you as you listened. Have Timothy spend some time next week polishing.

Be sensitive. As Timothy works on his testimony, he may see that his life has not changed. Timothy may think he is a Christian and isn't. Or he may see that he needs to become a Christian. If so, review Book 1, Lesson 6 with him.

Next Steps:

1. *Refer to the "Ten Most Wanted" card from the back of Book 2. Inquire about the people on the list, who they are, how long a relationship has existed, what concerns there may be. Book 3, Chapter 2 deals with the "Ten Most Wanted" in more detail.*
2. *Close by praying together for the people on each of your lists. Pray that God would give you the opportunity to "raise flags" and share "faith stories" and, eventually, your testimony with those on your list.*
3. *When you complete this chapter, give Timothy Book 3 and go over the table of contents, highlighting what you will learn together. Set day, date and time for your next meeting.*
4. *Update diary.*

3 Living with Power

INTRODUCTION TO BOOK 3

The oil lamp on the cover illustrates Christ's instruction for us to be "salt and light" in this dark world. To live with power requires total reliance on the Holy Spirit, who is our power source for this kind of life. The Bible also refers to the Holy Spirit as the oil in our lamp. Book 3 examines the process of depending completely on the Holy Spirit, prayer, quiet times, community, character, suffering and God's will. Scripture memory continues, as well as a deeper grasp of God's eternal, unchangeable truths.

BOOK 3, CHAPTER 1: Digging into the Bible

THE BIG IDEA

To assist Timothy in gaining a greater understanding of the purpose of the Bible — what it means on a personal level, and how to begin to study it on his/her own.

KEY TEACHING POINTS

1. The Bible is God's message to man on who He is, how we are to live and His promises to us.
2. In order to gain deeper understanding and value from the Bible, we need to have a balance of hearing, reading, studying, memorizing and meditating upon it.
3. When studying or meditating on a passage, it helps to ask the questions: What? So what? Now what?

TEACHING OUTLINE

I. WHAT IS THE PURPOSE OF THE BIBLE? PAGE 4
The Bible exists to teach, rebuke, correct and train us.

II. HOW DOES THE BIBLE HELP ME? PAGES 5–8
The Bible gives us instruction and illustrates how we are to live
the Christian life.

III. WHAT WILL I DO WITH THE BIBLE? PAGES 9–10
The Bible will help train us how to live only if we apply what it says.

MEMORY VERSE:
Memorize 2 Timothy 3:16,17 and review together.

ADDITIONAL DISCUSSION QUESTIONS AND ILLUSTRATIONS

Read through the quotes on page 3 and share your reactions to them.

Review
In Book 1 (page 11) and Book 2 (page 34) review the sections dealing with
2 Timothy 3:16. Discuss the four principles outlined, and ask Timothy to explain.

Page 4
Q: "What is so significant about this verse? Why?"
Q: "How has your view of this passage changed?"

Hebrews 4:12 says that the Word of God is active, living and sharper than
a two-edged sword…
Q: "What does this mean to you?"

Answers for chart on Psalm 19:7-11

Page 5

Law	Perfect	Refreshes me spiritually
Statutes	Trustworthy	Gives me wisdom
Precepts	Right	Brings joy to my heart
Commands	Radiant	Gives light to my eyes
Ordinances	Sure, righteous, when kept	Warns me, gives great reward
	More precious than gold,	
	Sweeter than honey.	

If Timothy had difficulty with the chart on Psalm 119, work through it together. Some of the attitudes and actions are interchangeable; the main emphasis is on the content of the verses, not filling in the chart perfectly.

Page 6

Discuss the significance of the sequence in Ezra 7:10 and its implications for living.

Page 7   *The Hand Illustration*
(Visual demonstration to illustrate getting a grip on God's Word)

THE HAND
AN ILLUSTRATION

Pick up the Bible with one hand. Transfer it over to the other hand, but try to hold it only by your little finger. It will naturally fall. Try again, this time holding it with the little finger and the thumb only. It can be grasped in this way, but can be easily pulled out of your grasp. (Have Timothy take the Bible out of your hand.) Then, demonstrate the increasing grip you have physically on the Bible as you add each finger along with the thumb. When all five fingers are gripping the Bible, Timothy will have a difficult time getting it out of your grasp. This visually demonstrates the spiritual principle of getting a strong grip on God's Word — it takes not just one or two of these means, but all five to ensure a sturdy grasp of God's Word. Meditation is the key to each of the other four.

Discuss with Timothy how to increase all five in his/her life.

Discuss prisoners of war, people in countries in which Bibles are forbidden, times of sickness and despair, times of temptation, when memorized Scripture was used by God to encourage, strengthen and sustain His children or you personally.

Page 8

Q: "What does it mean when the Bible says, 'Then you will be prosperous and successful?'" (Joshua 1:8)

Q: "Does it always mean financial/physical success?"

Discuss other ways success comes as a result of memorizing God's Word. Example: Joseph was in prison for 17 years, yet the Bible says that "the Lord was with him and he prospered." He was thrown in jail for refusing to commit adultery with his boss' wife — yet ultimately he was given a place of great honor.

Q: "Can we expect this kind of result? Why? Why not?"

BOOK THREE

Before discussing Psalm 1, take a blank sheet of paper and crayons. Ask Timothy to draw a tree that would depict his/her life. Ask Timothy to explain the drawing. Now ask Timothy to draw the tree described in Psalm 1. Compare and contrast the differences.

Page 9

Prior to your time together, draw a picture of a tree in which the top half of the page is the tree, but the bottom half to three-quarters of the page is taken up by the roots. Make the roots strong and deep, right beside a stream. Put some kind of fruit on the tree. Explain that everyone wants the beautiful fruit, but most only work on the top half — what can be seen. It takes strong roots to provide the nourishment necessary for growth.

Note: Ask the following questions regarding this whole chapter of "Digging into the Bible:"
Q: "What did it say?"
Q: "What did it say to me?"
Q: "What will I do about it?"

Key Questions
Close with a discussion of the key issues Timothy has picked up as a result of the study.

Page 10

Next Steps:

1. *Pray together*
2. *Assign next chapter, set day, date and time for your next meeting.*

Tips on what a quiet time is, how to have one, and practical suggestions are covered at the end of chapter 2, Communicating with God. If Timothy is having questions about a quiet time, you may want to cover pages 21-23 in Book 3 at this time or defer the discussion until the following week.

BOOK 3, CHAPTER 2: Communicating with God

THE BIG IDEA

To help Timothy learn that prayer is the primary means of communicating with God, highlight it's benefits and demonstrate how to develop a more effective prayer life.

KEY TEACHING POINTS

1. Praying may consist of praise, thanksgiving, confession, and asking for help for oneself and others.
2. God answers all prayer — yes, no, or wait; yet there are some conditions for prayer (belief, pure heart, unselfish motives, etc.).
3. A "Ten Most Wanted" prayer list helps us focus on people we desire to come to Christ.
4. A quiet time is a vital and special time alone with God to hear from Him, share our hearts and be directed by Him.

TEACHING OUTLINE

I. WHAT ARE THE ESSENTIALS OF PRAYER? **PAGES 14–16**
There are five essentials of prayer: praise, thanksgiving, confession, prayer for others and for ourselves.

II. WHAT ARE THE BENEFITS OF PRAYER? **PAGE 17**
Prayer relieves our anxiety and stress and allows us to live a life of inward peace.

III. FOR WHOM DO I PRAY? **PAGES 18–21**
We are instructed to pray especially for the unsaved Jews; for more "workers" to share their faith; for those in authority; and for those who mistreat us.

IV. HOW DO WE SPEND TIME WITH GOD? **PAGES 21–23**
We are to spend a quiet time, alone with God, for adoration, confession, thanksgiving and supplication.

 **MEMORY VERSE:**
Memorize Philippians 4:6,7.

BOOK THREE

ADDITIONAL DISCUSSION QUESTIONS AND ILLUSTRATIONS

Begin with a review of the memory verses.

Page 13

Warm Up
If Timothy has circled "f. Other", ask what "other" means. If Timothy is a poor communicator, or is experiencing problems in communication in certain relationships, this lesson may be difficult. Go at a measured pace and allow God to heal and reveal new insights in this area.

The "Warm Up" paragraph may stir some painful memories. Be sensitive. Discern whether Timothy needs some time to talk about any issues.

To avoid getting sidetracked, encourage Timothy that continuing to dip deep into God's Word, especially in this area of communication and prayer, will also have an overflow effect in other relationships. Book 4 is an option at this point if there are deep marital problems that surface.

Page 14

Q: "What is the difference between confident praying and presumptuous praying? How can we come to God in confidence and humility at the same time?"

Discuss the types of prayer and Timothy's response to each.

Page 15

Share your disappointing answers to prayer and what you have learned as a result.

"Much of our difficulty as seeking Christians stems from our unwillingness to take God as He is and adjust our lives accordingly. We insist upon trying to modify Him and to bring Him nearer our own image. The flesh whimpers against the inexorable sentence and begs like Agag for a little mercy, a little indulgence of its carnal ways. It is no use. We can get a right start only by accepting God as He is and learning to love Him for what He is. As we go on to know Him better we shall find it a source of unspeakable joy that God is just what He is. Some of the most rapturous moments we know will be those we spend in reverent admiration of the Godhead. In those holy moments the very thought of change in Him will be too painful to endure."

A. W. Tozer, *The Pursuit of God*

"What is prayer? Prayer is not so much an act as it is an *attitude* — an attitude of *dependency,* dependency upon God. Prayer is a confession of creature weakness, yea, of helplessness. We do not say that this is *all* there is in prayer; it is not. But it *is* the essential, the primary element in prayer... Therefore, prayer is the very opposite of *dictating* to God."

A. W. Pink *The Sovereignty of God*

Discuss various phrases in the Lord's Prayer. For example, what does it mean to ask God to forgive our debts/trespasses in the same way we forgive others? **Q:** "Do you really want God to forgive you the same way you forgive others?"

Page 16

Q: "Is there one area of your life about which you would like to experience this peace?" Is so, share it.

Page 17 Martin Luther said, "Prayer is not overcoming God's reluctance, but laying hold of His willingness."

If Timothy prayed through Ephesians 3:14-21 for someone, suggest that he write a note telling them so.

Page 18

Take time to discuss and pray for the people you have on your lists.

Page 19

Prayer list
If you have a prayer list, or a personal plan for praying for people, share it with Timothy.

Page 20

Quiet Time
Cover this section thoroughly. Share your personal ups and downs, as well as practical tips regarding your quiet time (time, place, what you do, etc.); encourage Timothy to find a plan that works.

Page 21

Q: "Do you currently have a plan for spending time with God?" (Help Timothy to be realistic about beginning or continuing a time with God).

Next Steps:

1. Discuss how the memory verse might apply to Timothy's life.
2. Set time, date and place for your next meeting.
3. Commit to encourage one another regarding your quiet times, sharing what has been meaningful to you.

BOOK 3, CHAPTER 3: Thriving in the Church

THE BIG IDEA

To underscore that God does not call us to be a "Lone Ranger," rather to be involved with one another through the fellowship of the church.

KEY TEACHING POINTS

1. The church, first and foremost, is all believers who make up the "body of Christ." Much of the teaching in the Bible refers to this definition of the church. It is often used interchangably to mean the local congregation or building on the corner.
2. The mission of the church is to reach outward to the lost and inward to embrace its own. This can easily be out of balance.
3. We need "one another" and the church provides a context for these kinds of relationships.
4. When selecting a local fellowship, be aware of denominational issues, know and examine the absolute, basic elements listed in this chapter.

TEACHING OUTLINE

I.   WHAT IS THE CHURCH?   **PAGES 26–28**
     The Greek word for "church" in the New Testament refers to
     all believers who make up the body of Christ.
II. WHAT DOES THE CHURCH DO?   **PAGES 28–29**
     The church is to take the message of Christ to the world and
     to be a place for fellowship with "one another" and for worship.

III. SHOULD I BE INVOLVED IN THE CHURCH? **PAGE 30**

We have no choice: we are a part of the church.

IV. HOW CAN I THRIVE IN THE CHURCH? **PAGES 31–33**

We can thrive as a result of maintaining sound doctrine, using our spiritual gifts to build the Body, protecting and shepherding the believers, and being committed and faithful to Christ.

MEMORY VERSE:

Memorize Colossians 1:18.

ADDITIONAL DISCUSSION QUESTIONS AND ILLUSTRATIONS

Page 25

Review all memory verses as you begin. Spend some time revisiting Timothy's church background, if necessary. You may want to read through notes in the diary for details that have already been shared, and add those revealed in this discussion for future reference.

If Timothy shares predominantly negative information regarding church at this point, ask if there were any positive aspects. If, on the other hand, Timothy shares only the positive, probe for any negative influences or experiences that may add to your understanding. Ask about parental and sibling church backgrounds as well.

Experiences will vary. Some may have never attended church, others only as a child, and still others may have been raised in a Christian home, but at some point may have rejected the faith. Timothy may presently be in a church that is not preaching the gospel or encouraging Christ-centered teaching and growth.

Be gentle and go slowly. Consider the possible reactions and feelings of Timothy's spouse, children and other family members as you discuss these issues. One new Christian was counseled by a well-meaning disciple-maker to leave one church immediately, even though the family was against it. It became a major reason for a subsequent divorce. Have the patience to consider all the factors.

The goal of this study is to allow Timothy to discover what God has revealed about the church and to pray that God will guide Timothy as the Scripture becomes more and more real. If Timothy's family is not Christian, or are lukewarm regarding spiritual growth, your role will be one of an encourager.

Church in Scripture

Page 26

This is a brief overview of some of the passages in the Bible regarding the church. It is not meant as an exhaustive, comprehensive study. The lesson is only intended to give Timothy a positive understanding of God's purpose for the church and a few practical guidelines.

Timetables aren't the issue: I Corinthians 12: 11-14

Page 27

Don't get hung up on "when does this happen?" Answers will vary. Instead, spend your time discussing the following section which deals with the summary of the church.

You might need to help Timothy with the matching section, "Under Construction." The blanks to the right are given for fuller explanation of each choice.

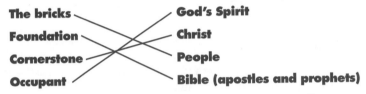

The bricks   **God's Spirit**
Foundation   **Christ**
Cornerstone   **People**
Occupant   **Bible (apostles and prophets)**

Q: "How has the local church ministered to you personally or someone you know? What is most meaningful to you of all the areas in which the church ministers?"

One Anothers

Page 29

Romans 15:7	**Accept one another**
Galatians 5:13	**Serve one another**
Galatians 6:2	**Carry one another's burdens**
Ephesians 4:2	**Bear with one another in love**
Ephesians 5:21	**Submit to one another out of reverence to Christ**
Philippians 2:3,4	**Consider others better than yourself**
Colossians 3:16	**Teach and admonish one another with all wisdom**
I Thessalonians 4:18	**Encourage each other**
I John 4:7	**Love one another**

Encourage Timothy to apply the above Scriptures at home, as well as at church. Discuss the implications of serving your spouse, accepting him/her unconditionally, etc.

Q: "What would your church be like if the people who attend would practice these principles?"

If Timothy is a workaholic or overachiever, there may be a need to encourage some balance in the number of church commitments, especially if there is little family time left.

No Lone Rangers
Work through the Scriptures together, sharing your insights. This section emphasizes the importance of being a part of a vibrant church fellowship.

Page 30

Q: "Have you had any experience with hypocrites? In what way? Did this color your view of the church?"

In I Corinthians 14:12 the Bible encourages excellence. Discuss how this spells out in practical terms regarding involvement within the church.

Page 31

Q: "How do we avoid perfectionism while pursuing excellence?"

Read Hebrews 10:24,25 together, then discuss what may keep people from attending church on a regular basis.

Identifying a Thriving Church
Q: "Do you feel that you are thriving in your church? How about your spouse? Children?"

Page 32

Be careful in advising Timothy in this area, especially if it may involve making changes. Pray. Walk through the discovery process together.

Next Steps:

1. *Encourage Timothy in the area of Scripture memory.*
2. *Assign the next chapter, write down day, date and time of your next meeting.*
3. *At home, update your diary regarding Timothy's church situation.*

BOOK 3, CHAPTER 4: Becoming a Person of Character

THE BIG IDEA

To understand that God desires us to become people with a depth of character. Who we are on the inside ultimately drives our behavior.

KEY TEACHING POINTS

1. **Developing character is a "moral struggle" that doesn't begin with us, but begins with Christ in us.**
2. **Character is forged in the fiery furnace of trials and difficulties.**
3. **Humility is the ultimate expression of character, through which God can have free reign in our lives.**
4. **Character begins with my view of God, is reflected in my values, and displayed in my behavior. It is a process that happens from the inside out; changing my behavior doesn't always change my view of God.**

TEACHING OUTLINE

MEMORY VERSE:
Memorize Romans 12:1-2.

ADDITIONAL DISCUSSION QUESTIONS AND ILLUSTRATIONS

Warm Up

Q: "What does the first quote mean to you 'Man will do in the presence of God what he will never do in the presence of men.?'"

Page 35 **Q:** "Why is humility essential to this?"

Share your answers to this section with Timothy.

Q: "What is your reaction to the fact that although we are a work in progress, it is not to be used as an excuse to continue to exhibit moral failures?"

Character and Fruit

Galatians lists the fruit of the Spirit ("character qualities the Holy Spirit has imparted to us.") They are the evidence that He indwells us — not that we

Page 36 will see any one of these lived out to perfection in our lives. But the difference between the work of the Holy Spirit in our lives and the "acts of the sinful nature" are obvious and diametrically opposed.

Read Galatians 5:16-21 with Timothy and compare and contrast the sinful nature's character qualities with those of the Spirit.

Q: "How does verse 24 in this passage say we deal with the sinful nature? How do we do this practically?"

Character Qualities

I Corinthians 15:58	**Perseverance, endurance**
I Thessalonians 5:8	**Gratefulness, thankful spirit**
James 2:8	**Love others as yourself**
Romans 13:8	**Pay all debts, love each other**
Matthew 7:12	**Respectful, considerate**
Colossians 3:13	**Forbearance, forgiving spirit**
I Peter 5:5	**Humble, submissive**
Matthew 5:8	**Purity**
I Corinthians 6:20	**Honor God with my body**
Hebrews 12:14	**Peacemaker; holy**
II Corinthians 9:7	**Cheerfully generous**
Proverbs 19:11	**Wise, patient, merciful**

Page 37

BOOK THREE

Page 38

Character Development
Q: "What does 2 Peter 1:3-11 say about the process of character development? What does verse 8 say in particular? Is there a time factor involved? Does this encourage you, discourage you?"

"Be transformed" in the Greek is *metamorphoo*. You might recognize the root of the word metamorphosis.

THE BUTTERFLY
AN ILLUSTRATION

There is a story of a young boy who came upon a cocoon from which a butterfly was struggling to free itself. The boy took pity on the agony of the butterfly's struggle and tried to help by cutting away the cocoon with a pair of scissors, not knowing that the struggle itself is designed to strengthen the wings and enable the butterfly to take flight. The butterfly emerged crippled and unable to fly.

If we are not careful, our efforts to shorten the struggles and lessen our pain or other's pain will cut short the process of our transformation into the likeness of Christ.
Q: "In what stage of development are you presently?

Page 39

The Seven Elements
The illustration is explained in detail in Jim Petersen's book *Lifestyle Discipleship*, Chapter 8. Reading this chapter would add insight into this lesson. In addition, *Living Proof II, Session 7* vividly portrays this process and explains it in greater detail.

Page 40

Past and Present Pain
Listen carefully and ask questions as Timothy shares.
Timothy may have difficulty with Romans 8:28 and Hebrews 12:7-11 if there was abuse as a child, or deeply painful experiences. Be gentle. Don't attempt to "heal" a deep wound with a Band-Aid or a pat answer. Listen. Share that our Heavenly Father never abuses us.

Page 41

Fill-in-the-blank
"The *testing* of your faith develops *perseverance*. *Perseverance* must finish its work so that you may be *mature and complete*."

Scriptures

Q: "Which has more to do with developing character: world view or behavior? Why?"

Pages 42-47

Cover all the Scriptures and questions on these pages carefully. Be honest with Timothy about your own life. Don't rush through this material.

"Accept the person, problems and all. Take failure in stride. Remember, failures are not the problem. It is the attitudes that produce the failures that require transforming. This work should be left to the Holy Spirit."
Jim Petersen

Next Steps:

1. *Review the memory verses.*
2. *Pray together.*
3. *Assign chapter 5, set date and time of next meeting.*
4. *Be available to Timothy this week for encouragement or support in these character issues.*

BOOK 3, CHAPTER 5: Pursuing Intimacy with God

THE BIG IDEA

To point out to Timothy that, above all else, God desires an intimate relationship with us — an ongoing, developing process that is often accompanied by adversity and suffering.

KEY TEACHING POINTS

1. **To have intimacy with God, we begin with getting to know God — who He is and what He does.**
2. **God loves us and pursues us to establish and maintain this intimacy with Him.**
3. **In God's presence, our reaction should be one of humility and "fearing Him." God works on us, and through us.**
4. **We will have one of two reactions to adversity and suffering: we may draw closer to God or we may flee from Him. Our response is crucial.**

BOOK THREE

TEACHING OUTLINE

I. WHO IS GOD? PAGES 50–51
What we believe about God is the most important thing about us.

II. HOW DOES GOD PURSUE US? PAGES 51–52
God has taken the initiative for the development of intimacy
with Him by becoming one of us and continually living within us.

III. HOW CAN WE GROW IN INTIMACY WITH GOD? PAGES 52–54
Intimacy with God hinges on our view of our ability and taking
advantage of His availability — it is a question of developing humility.

IV. HOW CAN WE FIND GOD IN OUR SUFFERING? PAGES 55–57
We discover God in our pain, suffering, and perseverance

MEMORY VERSE:
Memorize Isaiah 41:10.

ADDITIONAL DISCUSSION QUESTIONS
AND ILLUSTRATIONS

Begin your time together in prayer. Share your need to experience greater intimacy with
God. Pray for Timothy.

Cartoon and Quotes
Q: "Why is the thought expressed in the first quote by J. I. Packer a
'staggering thing?'"

Page 49

Q: "In your opinion, why is 'what we believe about God…the most
important thing about us?'"

Pages *What's in a Name?*
50–51 **Q:** "Which of the names listed is most meaningful to you? Why?"

It has been said we should be characterized by the direction, not by the
perfection, of our walk. Describe the direction of your walk — toward or
away from God."

Pages Read through John 15 with Timothy after covering the questions and para-
53–54 graphs on this page. Discuss it briefly. Encourage Timothy to read through
John 15 every day for the next week and jot down thoughts or insights.

**Pages
55-57**

Discuss questions and illustrations in detail.

If Timothy is experiencing a time of crisis or suffering, be gentle and patient. Allow the Holy Spirit to minister the Word to his heart and soul. Cover these questions and verses and allow Timothy to wrestle with the principles presented. Remind Timothy that it is not whether we understand or even "like" what Scriptures say, but whether we "surrender" to God and the truth He reveals. Understanding follows surrender.

Page 56

Describe a difficulty or trial you may be going through.
Q: "Which choice are you personally making?"

It is important to remember that many times our first response to situations is "why." It is often a process of time and the Holy Spirit's work within that changes our question from "why" to "what do you want me to learn from this?"

Next Steps:

1. *Review Isaiah 41:10. Suggest that Timothy go to sleep at night reviewing and meditating on this verse.*
2. *Point out the list of books on page 58 and recommend others that have been helpful to you.*
3. *Assign chapter 6. Make an appointment for your next meeting.*
4. *Pray for God's comfort, strength, and leading for Timothy.*
5. *Close with the reflection on page 58.*

BOOK 3, CHAPTER 6: Knowing God's Will

THE BIG IDEA

To understand that God has a plan and purpose for each of us. It is not a matter of having God rubber stamp our plan, rather, a matter of participating in His purposes.

KEY TEACHING POINTS

1. God has a plan and purpose for every one of His children. He has a universal purpose which includes everyone: to love Him, worship Him, be a witness for Him, to be thankful, abstain from immorality, etc.

BOOK THREE

2. **His unique will for us begins as we surrender our will and desires and fully follow Christ.**
3. **God is as interested in our hearts and how we proceed as He is in what we do.**
4. **A right relationship with God is essential to hearing God's direction for us moment by moment.**

TEACHING OUTLINE

I. **DOES GOD HAVE A PLAN?**   **PAGE 60**
God has an intimate plan for you and an ultimate plan for the world.

II. **KNOWING GOD'S WILL FOR EVERYONE.**   **PAGE 61**
The Bible contains the essence of God's will for mankind.

III. **DISCERNING GOD'S WILL**   **PAGES 62–64**
Through prayer, the study of the Word, and wise counsel we can discern God's will for us.

IV. **KEEPING THE CHANNELS CLEAR.**   **PAGES 65–67**
Sin and a lack of accountability can bring confusion to direction in life.

MEMORY VERSE:
Memorize Proverbs 3:5,6.

ADDITIONAL DISCUSSION QUESTIONS AND ILLUSTRATIONS

Begin with a discussion of the quotes on page 59.

Warm Up
Discuss Timothy's one question to God and it's significance.

Page 59

After discussing all the questions, ask Timothy which of the "it is always God's will for you…" statements are difficult for him/her to obey; which ones are being obeyed, disobeyed?

Page 61
Recommend that Timothy write out a gratitude list every day for a week and thank God for the things on the list.

Discuss the J. I. Packer quote on page 61.

Page 61

Shaded Box
Read through the shaded box carefully together. Use specifics from your own lives to discuss these principles.

Page 64 **Q:** "What significance for your own life does this have?"

If Timothy has not answered this section, ask questions to discern a particular decision he may be facing at this point. Don't give into the temptation to "tell" Timothy what God's will is. Keep asking questions that will allow Timothy to discover how God is leading.

Pages 66-67

Discuss the response Timothy has written at the top the page.

Page 68

Next Steps:

1. *Review Proverbs 3:5,6 and Isaiah 41:10.*
2. *Pray for God's guidance for the various decisions you are both facing at this time.*
3. *Take one session or make another appointment to review all the verses from the previous lessons.*
4. *Give Timothy Book 4, assign chapter 1. Go over the table of contents in advance.*

BOOK THREE

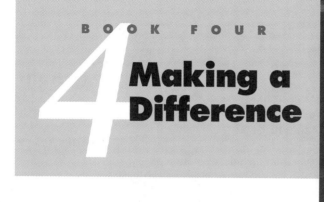

BOOK FOUR

4 Making a Difference

The cover of Book 4 of an open door represents our gateway to others — our families, co-workers, friends, the world. Christ said, "I am the door; if anyone enters by me he will be saved..." John 10:9. <u>Making a Difference</u> investigates the specifics of applying Scriptural principles in all our relationships by becoming "living proof" of who Christ is and what He has done and is doing in our lives. Marriage, work, money, maturity, life purpose and worldview are the topics of in-depth study. It moves Timothy from a simpler, topical study of Scripture to learning how to study Scripture inductively on his own.

BOOK 4, CHAPTER 1: Bringing It Home

THE BIG IDEA

To cause Timothy to examine relationships and align attitudes and actions with Biblical principles — specifically in the area of marriage and family.

KEY TEACHING POINTS

1. **Problems in our marriage relationship often reflect corresponding problems in our relationship to Christ and vice versa.**
2. **Marriage is much like a fire — without ongoing attention it will die out.**
3. **In order for a marriage to grow, we need to know how to fight fairly, handle sexual issues, deal with spiritual differences and resolve money issues.**
4. **To admire and praise your spouse daily is like watering a flower and seeing it bloom into full beauty.**

TEACHING OUTLINE

I. RELATIONSHIPS PAGES 4-11
Five keys to oneness in marriage include: love of your wife, respect of your husband, humbling of yourself, understanding differences/meeting needs of the other, and "fanning the flame."

II. REALITY PAGES 12-17
Four keys to living happily ever after include: resolution of conflict, development and protection of sexual intimacy, dealing with spiritual differences, and handling money.

III. REFLECTIONS PAGE 18
Practical suggestions are given for improving your family and marriage relationships.

MEMORY VERSE:
Memorize Ephesians 5:32,33.

ADDITIONAL DISCUSSION QUESTIONS AND ILLUSTRATIONS

Begin your time together by reading the quotes on the top of page 3.

Family Matters
Timothy's answer to this question at the top of page 4 will open the door for further discussion regarding family background and issues. Listen carefully. Past and present hurts and problems may make this session a particularly difficult one. Be sensitive and go slowly.

Page 4

Work through the positive and negative columns at the bottom of page 4. Discuss areas of struggle or change at the top of page 5.

Genuine Love
Read Ephesians 5:21-33 out loud. Discuss the questions. Look at Philippians 2:1-11 to see how Christ loved the church in more detail. Discuss other ways Christ demonstrated His love for the church and gave Himself up for her.

Page 5

A Profound Mystery
Ephesians 5:32 says that marriage is a profound mystery. God compares the marriage relationship to that of Christ and the church.
Page 6
Q: "With this in mind, of what significance is your relationship with your spouse to God?"

If the word "submission" was used as an excuse for abuse in Timothy's background, it may take some time to work through this. Taking all of the verses in context, especially verse 21, will give a balanced view of this truth.

It's all Greek

Page 7

The Greek word for submission is *hupotasso*, which is primarily a military term, meaning "to rank or arrange under", denoting to subject oneself, to obey, to be subject to.

The Greek word for "humility" is *tapeinos* primarily signifying "low-lying" and is always used in a good sense in the New Testament. Synonyms for humility are meekness, mildness, modesty, submissiveness. The opposite of humility is arrogance or pride. This is referring mainly to an inner attitude which results in humble external behavior and actions.

Q: "What is the difference between genuine humility and being a doormat or victim?"

Weaker Partner

Page 8

The word in I Peter 3:7 referring to the wife as the weaker partner alludes to bodily or physical strength, in the sense that most men are physically larger and stronger than their wives.

Q: "How could you begin to meet one of the needs of your spouse? Child? Family member? Friend?" discuss this section thoroughly.

Pages 8-9

Assessing Needs

Get a copy of the book, *Top Ten Intimacy Needs,* by Dr. David Ferguson and Dr. Don McMinn and work through the various exercises they suggest, asking specific questions about the needs that surface. Book 1 of Operation Timothy, *Finding the Way,* page 67 gives a fuller listing of basic needs that all humans have. Review these as you prepare for this lesson.

Pages 10-11

Many issues may surface as you discuss availability and priorities. Whether Timothy is a workaholic, is divorced, remarried, or single will determine how much time you spend talking through this section. Evaluate how you are doing as leaders with your own family.

BOOK FOUR

Family Feud

Proverbs 13:10 says, "*Pride* only breeds quarrels, but *wisdom* is found in those who *take advice*."

Pages 12-13

Q: "How does this apply in marriage? Do you apply passages like this to yourself or to others? In what way?"

Using Scripture as a means to judge or berate others instead of applying it to yourself creates more, not less, conflict in a relationship. Only as each person takes personal responsibility for his own attitudes, actions, and reactions can there be conflict resolution. You are not responsible for how your spouse decides to respond to Scripture, only for your own response.

Resources for Conflict Resolution:
The Anger Workbook by Drs. Les Carter and Frank Minirth, has inventories to help a person evaluate his levels and types of anger and anger management.

Happiness is a Choice by Drs. Minirth and Meier, deals with depression, but has a valuable section on handling anger and getting rid of grudges which can be applied in every relationship, not just marriage.

Q: "What is one thing you can do this week to take the initiative in resolving one conflict?"

Page 14

Be Sensitive

Take care as you work through this chapter. Many people today have been affected by divorce, death, abuse and other kinds of brokenness and wound-edness. Both the abused and the abuser need understanding and Christ's forgiveness. Sometimes the process of forgiving others is a lengthy one. Be patient.

Pages 14-16

Dealing with Spiritual Differences

If Timothy has experienced antagonism when sharing his newfound faith, gently ask about past actions or attitudes that may have contributed to the response of the other person. If forgiveness is in order, the ball is in Timothy's court to begin the process.

Pages 16-17

I Peter 2 and 3:1-9 is an excellent passage to meditate upon as you prepare to meet with Timothy. Read and discuss the verses preceding I Peter 3:1-9 in I Peter 2 with Timothy.

Next Steps:

1. *Pick one of the suggestions on page 18 and apply it this week with a child, spouse, parent, brother or sister.*
2. *Recommend the reading list at the bottom of page 19 and add any others you wish.*
3. *Review Ephesians 5:32-33 once again before you close.*
4. *Pray together that God will continue to give grace to love and respect your spouse.*
5. *Assign chapter 2; set day, date, and time.*

BOOK 4, CHAPTER 2: Taking it to Work

THE BIG IDEA

To help Timothy understand a proper view of work as a platform to demonstrate to others the excellency of Christ. It is essential to keep balance in our daily lives between work, home, and our daily walk with God.

KEY TEACHING POINTS

1. **God is our Provider; our worth and value do not come from our work. We don't work to make a living, we work because God commands it. It is an ideal arena to demonstrate the life of Christ as an insider to our families, friends and co-workers.**
2. **God never tells us how much to work; however, He does tell us that we must work, and that it always should be done to honor Christ.**
3. **Be careful of overworking — it destroys relationships and is not a means of gaining significance.**

TEACHING OUTLINE

I. **ATTITUDES TOWARDS WORK**   **PAGES 22-24**
   God has ordained work for us.
II. **ACTIONS AS WE WORK**   **PAGE 25**
   God has saved us to serve Him in a strategic location — on the job!

BOOK FOUR

III. EXAMPLE OF DANIEL   **PAGES 26–27**

God's desire is that we hold our posts in enemy territory as a
witness for Him.

IV. OVERLOAD   **PAGES 27–28**

Overwork is damaging to our health and our relationships.

 MEMORY VERSE:

Memorize Colossians 3:23.

ADDITIONAL DISCUSSION QUESTIONS AND ILLUSTRATIONS

Working through Gordon Adams' *Why Go to Work?* booklet would be helpful for this
session with Timothy. It goes into greater detail on each section of this chapter. You may
order it through CBMC by calling 1-800-575-2262.

Page 21

Cartoon and Quotes
Read and discuss the quotes and the cartoon on page 21 as you begin, then
work through the Warm Up section as usual.

**Pages
22-24**

Attitudes Toward Work
Use the Notes space on page 30 to list a summary of the attitudes God desires
us to have toward our work from the passages on these pages. Use this a prayer
list for the coming week, asking God to change your attitudes to conform more
and more to His. Your list might look something like this:

*Work is good, but difficult
We work to earn eternal food, not physical food
God is my Provider, my Resource for provision
Work enough to share with others in need
etc.*

My goal: That my daily life may win respect for Christ and that I will depend
on God to provide.

Page 23

Discuss questions on Philippians 4:19.

Where Do We Belong?

Page 25

Most new Christians need to be encouraged to stay where they are in their jobs. However, each person's situation will be unique. It may be that Timothy does need to consider another job or work opportunity. Discern the underlying attitudes and motives, if possible. Encourage patience, waiting on God.

Persecution vs. Personal Problems

Page 26

While there is persecution for our faith, some may claim martyr status when in reality there are other problems going on, such as mediocrity of work, bad attitudes toward employer or co-workers, undependability, etc. Giving a full day's effort for a full day's wage is God's standard and doing it in such a way as to display God's excellence, love and character.

On the other hand, we also should not be intimidated when it comes to sharing our faith as Daniel did.

Pages 27-28

If you or Timothy have not read Dr. Richard Swenson's book, *Margin*, and you are struggling with an overload of work and other commitments, this would be a good time to pick up a copy and read it. You will find excellent material for discussion in its pages.

Read and discuss the quote in the circle.

Next Steps:

1. *Pray through the things you both listed under "Key" question at the bottom of page 28.*
2. *Assign chapter 3 (This study may take 2 or 3 sessions); set day, date and time.*
3. *Close with the quote on page 30.*

BOOK 4, CHAPTER 3: Handling Money Wisely

THE BIG IDEA

To understand that there is nothing in our lives revealing our hearts more clearly than the way we handle our finances.

KEY TEACHING POINTS

1. God owns it all and wants us to be faithful stewards of what He gives to us.

2. God looks at our hearts as we handle money and will judge us accordingly.

BOOK FOUR

3. **Our giving reveals much about our heart attitude toward money and toward God.**
4. **Without a budget, we will tend to be casual and careless with our funds.**

TEACHING OUTLINE

MEMORY VERSE:

Memorize and review I Chronicles 29: 11-12.

ADDITIONAL DISCUSSION QUESTIONS AND ILLUSTRATIONS

Begin with a discussion of the quotes on page 31. Inquire what comfort level Timothy has in discussing this area of life with you. Be sensitive not to invade personal privacy by offering to be available on whatever level.

Because I Chronicles 29:11,12 clearly states that God is in control and sovereign over this area of money and wealth, Timothy may struggle with anger towards God because of a current financial situation. Listen. Share out of your own struggles. Invite Timothy to continue to look at the Scriptures to see what God wants to teach you both about the issues of finances.

Page 32

Page 33

Proverbs are not commands, but wise principles that are generally true. There are exceptions. It is especially important not to judge another believer's character by the level of success or wealth he possesses. Many Christians who were failures in the world's eyes were great men and women of God with godly character.

I Timothy 6:6-10 states the positive alternative to the love of money is "godliness with contentment."

Q: "What specific things describe this kind of lifestyle? Are you content with the food and clothing God provides? Is your life characterized by an attitude that you brought nothing into this world, and you can take nothing out of it?"

Q: "Have you experienced grief because of some poor decisions or "get-rich-quick" schemes? Are you easily enticed by these kind of offers to make a lot of money quickly?"

Q: "What is your reaction to the quote, 'There is nothing we handle that reveals the heart inside us like the way we handle money'"?

When discussing Matthew 6:24, read through the rest of the verses in that chapter. Discuss the relationship between our value to God and His provision for us. Also, discuss the issue of worry and what God says about it, particularly in regards to money, provision, etc. Note the phrase "how much more" in Matthew 6.

Page 34

Love of Money
Many Christians battle with the love of money and the desire to be rich. But there are some who deny themselves even basic needs for various unhealthy reasons. Balance is needed — Paul says that he has experienced both plenty and need and has learned contentment in each situation. The key word is "learned." The goal is progress, not perfection. Pray about the present relationship between *your* money and *your* heart.

Page 36

God's provision
Share faith stories of how God has sustained and provided for you or other Christians in times of need. You may want to cite the life of George Mueller, an Englishman who was used of God to establish an orphanage totally by faith, sharing his needs only with God through prayer.

Pages 37-42

Putting Principles into Practice
If Timothy has not completed this section, work through it together. Spend time talking about the difficult areas and the stresses involved in managing money. If you, as a leader, have never done this for yourself or your family, you may want to get the tapes and workbook from Christian Financial Concepts listed at the end of this section. In addition, Crown Ministries 12-week group study is an excellent resource for you and your spouse.

Realistic Goals

Q: "Do you have a budget? How are you using it?"

Page 42 Most people are not realistic when setting new financial goals and the time frame in which to accomplish them.

Next Steps:

1. *Plan to join a Crown Ministries study when feasible.*
2. *Assign chapter 4; set day, date and time of next meeting.*
3. *Pray for God's wisdom, and for courage and perseverance to please Him in the way you handle money.*
4. *Meditate on the reflections quote on page 44 this week.*

BOOK 4, CHAPTER 4: Moving Toward Maturity

THE BIG IDEA

To understand the "critical" process of spiritual maturity and how it applies to Timothy.

KEY TEACHING POINTS

1. **Spiritual growth is a life-long process.**
2. **Evangelism is not an event, but a process of sowing, cultivating and harvesting over a period of time.**
3. **Discipleship is ongoing, starting with spiritual birth, continuing through spiritual childhood, adolescence and adulthood. The goal is Christ-likeness.**
4. **We are called by God to live out these principles as a lifestyle, not as an activity or program.**
5. **God calls us to a life of fruitfulness — spiritual multiplication and reproduction.**

TEACHING OUTLINE

MEMORY VERSE:

Memorize 2 Timothy 2:2.

ADDITIONAL DISCUSSION QUESTIONS AND ILLUSTRATIONS

Review the memory verses together as you begin. Then discuss the cartoon and quotes on page 45.

CBMC has produced two dramatic video series called Living Proof I and II that illustrate the process of "Moving Toward Maturity." Viewing these would be the best preparation for covering the material in this study. You might consider the studies as a next step for Timothy as you wrap up the Operation Timothy study. Discussion and leader's guides accompany each video session. The story depicts several couples and singles as they deal with the issues of everyday life, spiritual growth, reaching others for Christ, and helping them to grow. The real-life, professional dramatic production is a compelling look at the maturing process in the Christian life.

Revisit the introductory pages of this guide and review the principles of effective discipleship.

Work through each of the questions, Scriptures and illustrations carefully with Timothy. Begin to plant the idea of Timothy taking someone else through Operation Timothy.

Pages 45-55 **Q:** "Where are you in the process of investing your life in the life of someone else?"

BOOK FOUR

Next Steps:

1. *Review 2 Timothy 2:2 and several other verses.*
2. *Pray together for two others with whom each of you can begin to do Operation Timothy. Use your "Ten Most Wanted" card to pray specifically.*
3) *Assign chapter 5; set time, date and place.*

BOOK 3, CHAPTER 5: Multiplying Your Life

THE BIG IDEA

To give Timothy a vision of being an Isaiah 60:22 person. Writing a life purpose statement increases a believer's sense of direction and fruitfulness.

KEY TEACHING POINTS

1. **There are certain non-negotiables to which God calls us: to love Him, love our neighbor, evangelize and disciple others.**
2. **God has a unique purpose for each individual that includes spiritual gifts, equipping, skills, history and temperament.**
3. **Spiritual reproduction does not simply happen, we need to make certain choices in our lives. A written purpose statement helps us say "yes" and "no" appropriately and become more fruitful.**

TEACHING OUTLINE

I. **UNDERSTANDING GOD'S PURPOSE FOR EVERYONE.** **PAGES 58–59**
   God's purpose for everyone is that they receive His gift of salvation through Christ.

II. **DISCOVERING GOD'S UNIQUE PURPOSE FOR ME.** **PAGES 59–63**
   God's specific will for us is revealed over time as we refine and clarify our purpose as we mature in our faith.

III. **ASSEMBLING A LIFE PURPOSE STATEMENT.** **PAGES 63–68**
   The development of a life purpose statement will give focus to priorities in your life.

MEMORY VERSE:
Memorize Isaiah 60:22.

ADDITIONAL DISCUSSION QUESTIONS AND ILLUSTRATIONS

Open your time with Timothy by reviewing Robert Munger's brief, but powerful booklet, *My Heart — Christ's Home.*

One size fits all

Q: "What does it mean to 'fear God and keep His commandments' to you personally? How do we act justly? Love mercy? Walk humbly?"

Page 58 **Q:** "How can we love our neighbor as we love ourselves? What does it really mean? How do we love ourselves?"

Spiritual Gifts

II Corinthians 10:12 says that comparison is a great hindrance to personal growth and usefulness.

Page 60 **Q:** "How has comparing yourself with others caused problems in your life?" One of the pitfalls in comparing ourselves with others is that we usually find someone who is in better shape physically, emotionally, spiritually, or financially. It leaves us feeling frustrated, inadequate and ungrateful. This is especially true in the area of spiritual gifts. Every believer is gifted by God and equipped to fulfill His unique, specific role for them. Discuss the spiritual gifts that you have both observed and discovered.

Balance

Q: "Do you feel that you have balance in your life of hearing, reading, studying, memorizing, and meditation of God's Word? What area needs to be strengthened?"

Page 61 **Q:** "Are you maintaining an accountable relationship with someone? Are you committed and active in a local fellowship of believers?"

Jot it down

You may need more room to do an adequate job here. Although by this time you know Timothy well, chances are you will discover even more during **Page 62** this exercise.

Personality Tests
If you have never taken a personality test to discover your temperament, the Birkman Method and the Performax Personality Profiles are two simple tests that are available. In addition, Team Resources has produced the **Marriage & Temperament Profile: A Guide for Creating Oneness in Your Marriage** which takes couples through the process as a means of improving communication. Call CBMC for more information.

Pages 62-63

Life Purpose Statement
Review Timothy's first draft. Share your own. Spend some time working through the sample purpose statements on pages 66-68, discuss the various parts, ask questions and give feedback to each other on areas you may have overlooked.

Pages 64-65

Next Steps:

1. *Review Isaiah 60:22. Discuss the meaning and significance of the verse.*
2. *Discuss the reflection quote on page 70.*
3. *Assign chapter 6; set day, date and time for the next meeting.*
4. *Close your time together in prayer for your "Ten Most Wanted List."*

BOOK 4, CHAPTER 6 Seeing the World God's Way

THE BIG IDEA

To help the believer discover and accept God's view of the world as his own, as well as to learn a method of studying God's Word in-depth on his own.

KEY TEACHING POINTS

1. **God wants us to be able to feed ourselves spiritually and then feed others.**
2. **God greatly loves the world, evidenced by Jesus Christ's prayer in John 17. We, too, are called to share His passion.**

CHAPTER SIX

TEACHING OUTLINE

I. HOW TO DO THE ADVANCED ABC BIBLE STUDY.   **PAGES 72-80**
The advanced ABC Bible study method gives us a means of
studying the Bible in-depth, on our own, through studying John 17.

II. HOW DOES JESUS VIEW THE WORLD?   **PAGE 81**
Jesus loves the people of this world.

III. SEEING THE WORLD GOD'S WAY.   **PAGE 82**
God desires that people know Him personally.

MEMORY VERSE:
Memorize Matthew 28:19,20 — a special challenge is to memorize several
verses from John 17 or the entire chapter.

ADDITIONAL DISCUSSION QUESTIONS AND ILLUSTRATIONS

Begin with a discussion of the quotes and the Warm Up section.

This lesson may take two sessions to cover the material adequately.

Page 71

Ask Timothy to read through each of the sections in pages 72-80. Share your
answers and discuss them. Keep encouraging Timothy to dig deeper. Your
goal is not to make Timothy dependent upon you, but whet his appetite and
to encourage further exploration and study.

Pages 72-80

This assignment is a big jump from what Timothy has been doing in the
weekly studies. Be patient. Offer help. Work through the sections together,
if necessary.

Additional Questions
These additional questions may not have come up in your discussion.
Discuss each with Timothy.

Page 81

Changing World View
Q: "How has your view of the world changed from your study of John 17?"

Page 82

BOOK FOUR

Next Steps:

1. *Review Matthew 28:19,20.*
2. *Set another time to review all the verses in Operation Timothy and discuss the suggestions on page 89. Encourage Timothy to make a commitment to another study, either with you or with a small group.*
3. *Be sure to complete the evaluation form on page 91, Book 4 with Timothy and fax or mail it to CBMC. We welcome any comments and feedback.*

CONCLUSIONS AND RECOMMENDATIONS

Congratulations! This part of your journey in getting to know God more intimately is finished, but this is only the beginning! Following are a few suggestions on the next steps you might take to help Timothy continue growing toward Christlikeness:

1. Study the OT Leader's Guide with Timothy:
   Take several weeks to go through the Operation Timothy Leader's Guide together. Begin praying about going through OT with another person or couple.

2. Help Timothy find his own Timothy:
   He should look for people who have the following characteristics:
   a. Heart for God
   b. Teachability
   c. Faithfulness
   d. Willingness to teach others
   Have Timothy make a list of people who have these qualities or the potential to develop them and pray for them. His "Timothy" may be a person he has had the privilege of leading to Christ, or a young, immature Christian, or even a non-Christian who is willing to explore God's Word, perhaps someone on his "Ten Most Wanted" List.

3. Encourage Timothy to continue to dig deep into God's Word.
   One idea is to do an Advanced ABC Bible study on the book of I Thessalonians. Also, have Timothy continue to memorize and meditate on Scripture (he may want to do the Navigators' Topical Memory System).

4. Together read Jim Petersen's books, *Living Proof,* and *Lifestyle Discipleship,* and Dr. Richard Swenson's book, *Margin.*

5. Lead Living Proof I and II group studies.

6. Lead a Crown Ministry group study.

7. Encourage Timothy to begin attending CBMC Family Conferences with his family. Have Timothy invite other couples to go along. Other seminars and training opportunities will greatly enhance and encourage his growth in the Lord.